PUFFI

THE CA
AND OTH

Here are nineteen fantastic stories of the coming of Christianity to the Pagan North, of battles fought and lost by the ancient and evil powers; of trolls and elves, bogeys and devils, wise men, witches and wizards against the holy army of Saints, Bishops and Priests.

Christians and Pagans don't always act as you would expect and the line between Good and Evil, old and new, is not always clear. A wizard goes to church, a bogey is kind and compassionate, a man marries the daughter of a troll, and a priest follows the devil to hell . . .

Susan Price retells these ancient legends which she has known from childhood. 'She tells them with a marvellous irony, a wry humour that is splendidly satisfying . . . a treat of style and imagination' – *Books and Bookmen*

Susan Price started writing for her own amusement when she was just fourteen and since then has written nine books for children and teenagers.

Another book by Susan Price

GHOSTS AT LARGE

THE CARPENTER

and Other Stories

Retold by Susan Price

PUFFIN BOOKS
in association with Faber and Faber

Puffin Books, Penguin Books Ltd, Harmondsworth, Middlesex, England
Viking Penguin Inc., 40 West 23rd Street, New York, New York 10010, U.S.A.
Penguin Books Australia Ltd, Ringwood, Victoria, Australia
Penguin Books Canada Limited, 2801 John Street, Markham, Ontario, Canada L3R 1B4
Penguin Books (N.Z.) Ltd, 182 190 Wairau Road, Auckland 10, New Zealand

First published by Faber and Faber 1981
Published in Puffin Books 1986

Made and printed in Great Britain by
Richard Clay Ltd, Bungay, Suffolk

Contents

The Wise Man in the Stone, and Thorhall's Vision

THERE once lived a man named Kodran, who had worshipped the old gods, Freyr and Freyja, Thor and Odin, all his life, as all his family before him had done; but during Kodran's lifetime the new faith of Christianity came to his country, and his son became converted to it. Kodran made no objections, but took an interest in the faith, and in the bishop who preached it, and, after a while, he was heard to say that he was impressed by the devotion of the Christians to their god and that, in his opinion, their bishop had the second sight because he gave his followers such good advice. He gave them such good advice, Kodran added, that he might have gone to the bishop himself if it were not for the fact that on his farm was a great stone in which lived a wise man who gave Kodran all the advice he needed, besides guarding his cattle, predicting the weather and foretelling the future.

What Kodran had said was repeated from one to another until the Christian bishop came to hear of it, and he was not pleased by the story of Kodran's wise man, and even less pleased by the account of the fine scarlet cloth and golden ornaments which the wise man wore. The bishop took prayer-books, and prayer-beads, and holy water, and he walked over to Kodran's farm and found the great stone. Then he began to pray, and to sing psalms, and to sprinkle holy water over the stone; to drive out the wise man who was his rival.

That night, as Kodran was asleep in his bed, he thought that he saw the wise man from the stone standing beside him, dressed in red and wearing gold finger-rings, and another ring of gold round his neck. But the wise man's face was swollen with weariness. "Kodran," the wise man said, "why are you allowing this stranger to treat me like this? He has banged on my walls, he has howled and screeched all day long, and he has poured boiling water over my house until my children cried out in pain. Make him go away, Kodran, and let us have peace."

Kodran woke then, and sat up quickly in bed, but the wise man vanished the very second Kodran's eyes opened, and he saw nothing but the blurred shapes of his furniture in the darkness, and heard no voice, but only the fire burning low and ashes falling. He sat awake for a while, thinking over his dream, but although he knew the Christian bishop was on his land, praying over the stone, he did not like to do anything about it because his son was now a Christian. Besides, he thought that the bishop would soon grow tired of his exorcism.

But the bishop went on praying, and, the next night, Kodran dreamt of the wise man again. He had taken off his golden ornaments, and his scarlet clothes were crumpled and stained. "Kodran, Kodran," he said, "when will this hammering, this shrieking, this torture of scalding water, be over? This man would drive me out of my home. I have always been helpful to you, Kodran; when will you make him stop? Make him go away, and let us have peace."

The next day Kodran remembered the dream, but he still did nothing, telling himself that if the bishop did not stop his praying and hymn-singing soon, he would make him stop; but Kodran waited too long. On the third night, the wise man came again, but now he was wearing a cloak of hard, black skin, and his face was pale, tired and ill.

"Kodran," he said, "we must go out from our stone, my family and I, and where shall we find another home now, with so many churches in the land, and with so much hymn-singing and bell-ringing? I fear that in the future, when we are tired and wish to rest, we will be driven on; when we are hungry and wish to stop and eat, we will be chased away; when we are cold and wish to warm ourselves, there will be no one who will let us come to their fire; and so we will wander always from place to place, homeless, betrayed by our protectors, Kodran, and with no salvation at our lives' ends. I wish sorrow on you, Kodran, who would not help me when I asked, even though I have always given you good advice, and guarded your house and your goods. You never knew bad luck or hard times while I was working for you, but, since this is my reward, you will never receive such service again as I gave you." And the wise man lifted his cloak of black skin across his face, and Kodran woke from his dream to find his farmhouse dark, empty and silent.

He never saw the wise man from the stone again, but he often remembered his last words, because from that night Kodran never had any luck. His servants stole from him, and were so careless of his property that he lost many cattle and sheep through disease; and his sons quarrelled with him over his property and made his life miserable; but, as his wealth and his hopes dwindled away, he became a Christian, and so gained life eternal.

It is also said that in Iceland, at the time Christianity was first brought to that island, there was living a man named Thorhall, who had second sight. He was found one day standing outside his farmhouse door, looking out over the country round about. When asked what was the matter, he shook his head sadly, and would not answer.

But a while later, when asked why he had looked so unhappy, he said, "I saw the hills opening, and I saw all the people of the hills gathering together their pots and pans and other belongings, and packing them into sacks, and all the time they were crying. When they had all their things on their backs, and had no more reason to stay, they came out from the hills, all of them, a great stream of them, and their journey brought them towards me. They were so many, and the noise of their feet dragging on the ground was so constant and so loud; and their wailing and calling out of farewells to the places they loved, so loud and so pitiful, that I cannot understand why every man, woman and child in Iceland did not see and hear them. They passed close to me, and I called out to their leader, asking them where they were going. 'Christ has come to Iceland,' he said to me, 'and we must leave. We must hurry away from the churches before they set the bells ringing, before the people begin praying and singing hymns. We must go far away, Thorhall, friend, and we can never return.' Then they passed me by and went on, all the long line of them, all the people of the hills. I watched them go, and it came to me that no one after me would ever see a sight such as that I was watching; that stories would be told of this, and it would be disbelieved; and that is why I am sad, for though we have gained Christ, what have we lost?"

The Carpenter

S T. CUTHMAN wished to do God's will by building a church, one of the first in the land, but he knew that the building of a church was a serious business, not to be approached without forethought and prayer. Nothing about it could be done carelessly, not the digging of the postholes, nor the cutting of the timber, nor, least of all, the choosing of the site, for the situation of the church must be one blessed by the Lord. It had been the practice of the heathens to let their devilgods choose the site of a new house or temple, and it seemed right to St. Cuthman to let the One True God choose the site of His new house of worship. Since there was so much country to choose from, Cuthman decided to travel from one place to another, never resting, until his God sent him some sign that he had reached the place where the church was to be built.

But St. Cuthman's plans were hindered by his mother, a very old woman whose teeth had all worn down to her gums long before, and whose watering eyes were like clouded glass. St. Cuthman looked at her as she sat by his fire, licking her gums and dabbing at her eyes, and knew that he could not leave her behind—yet he was not going to let her keep him from his duty. That night he prayed for advice, and received it; and, the next morning, he wrapped his mother up well, loaded her into a wheelbarrow, and began his long journey.

He pushed his mother, in the wheelbarrow, from Devon to Sussex, and over all that distance, and in all that time, Cuthman received no sign from God that any of the places they passed were suitable for church-building. But, as he approached the town of Steyning, the wheelbarrow broke and let his poor old mother fall on to the ground with a crash and a squeal. There were some men making hay in a nearby field and they saw it all—the bony, lanky man struggling to push along the little old lady bundled into the barrow, and the shock and the legs in the air and the shouting—and the haymakers all began to laugh, setting down their tools in order to point and jeer.

St. Cuthman was angry. "Laugh man," he shouted at them, "but weep Heaven." Immediately rain began to fall on that one field, hard rain which broke down the standing grass and drenched what had been cut. At the exact borders of the field, on each of its sides, the downpour stopped; and the hay-makers stopped laughing. They gaped as they saw all their work being spoiled, and they called out to St. Cuthman, begging him to forgive them and to take away his spell . . . but it was too late. St. Cuthman had mended the barrow with withies from the hedge, and had pushed his mother away along the road.

He had gone only a few hundred yards when the barrow broke again, and dropped his old mother into the wet grass. Then St. Cuthman saw that this was his sign. Here was where he was meant to stop and build his church. At once he started work and made a small shelter where he and his mother could live while the church was erected. Inside the shelter that night they ate and prayed, and the next day St. Cuthman began to build his church.

He cut the timber, and cleared the ground, and levelled it, and marked out the ground-plan, and dug the postholes. In fact, all went very well until he came to the fitting together of the timbers. Then he found that he had no skill at carpentry. He discovered that he had not the right tools, and when he managed to beg, borrow, buy or commandeer the tools he needed, he did not know how to use them. Saws would not cut straight for him; hammers, in his hands, would hit nothing but his thumbs; and whatever he measured either stretched or shrank while his back was turned, and would not fit the posthole or joint he had made for it. Weeks passed, and still the church was nothing more than a pattern of postholes in the ground.

Then, walking along the road, there came a man with a bag of tools on his back. He stopped to watch the Saint's fretful work, and St. Cuthman scowled at him. The stranger was neither young nor old, not very tall, but strong-looking, as if he were used to walking for long distances and working with his hands and arms and back. Long dark hair hung over his shoulders, and he had a black beard. He asked the Saint what he was doing.

"I am trying to build a church," said the Saint, and sweated with embarrassment under the stranger's stare, and grew clumsy, and dropped things.

The stranger left the road and began to wander among the pieces, large and small, of discarded timber. He said, "What you need is a carpenter."

"I don't have a carpenter," said the Saint. "I have

one old mother, and she is worse at woodwork than I am."

"I am a carpenter," said the stranger. "I have all my tools here." And he jerked his thumb over his shoulder at the bag on his back.

St. Cuthman stared at him. "What do you want in exchange for staying here and working on my church?" he asked.

The carpenter smiled. "Oh, let's finish it before we talk of that," he said, and dropped the bag of tools from his shoulders, and took off his coat.

That day, and for many days after, Cuthman, although a Saint, ran about at the orders of the carpenter, for this carpenter was a master of his craft. Every one of his tools had been worn to the grasp of his hand, and, once in his hand, they seemed to move of their own accord, he used so little effort. The palms of his hands were covered with thick callouses, not, as Cuthman's were, with blisters; and he would stroke a piece of wood he had worked on with loving attention, as if trying to remember every detail of its texture, grain and scent. He would fit it to its brother-beam, and they would fit as close as if they had grown together. The wallposts were sunk, the planks for the wall were fixed together with their pegs of wood, the roof-beams were raised; and through all the work the carpenter smiled, and often sang and whistled, moving about so quickly that often the Saint could not keep up with him as he tried to hand him tools. The Saint often rebuked the workman for behaving in such a frivolous manner while engaged in God's work, but the carpenter only replied that he was so happy to be in work again that he could not keep quiet. St. Cuthman tut-tutted, and frowned whenever he heard some dance-tune being hummed, but he was careful not to offend the carpenter in case he went away before the church was finished.

At last it was finished. The two men, the carpenter and the Saint, stood and looked at it, and both sighed with satisfaction.

"Now, my dear good fellow," said the Saint, turning to his helper. "You must tell me how I can pay you. Shall I spend my life in praying for your soul? Is there some sin of which you wish to be absolved? Is there any advice I can give you, or some theological difficulty which I can explain?"

The carpenter smiled, picked up his bag of tools and swung them to his shoulder. "No, Cuthman," he said. "But keep my laws." And then he vanished.

Of all the early saints, there was none more humble than St. Cuthman.

The Priest and the Neckan

THERE was once a preacher, who, travelling from one town to another, climbed a steep mountain track beside a stream. Reaching the summit of a rise, he came upon a deep pool caught in a hollow, and, at the same moment that he glimpsed the deep water, he heard music and singing: pleasant sounds which offended his mood. He stopped and looked round to see where the sounds came from, and he saw, seated above the pool on a rock, a Neckan, the spirit of the pool, looking like a young man with long, wet hair, playing on the golden harp which all Neckans possess, and singing in a strong, clear, pleasing voice.

The preacher was even more offended to see this godless creature amusing itself so contentedly, and he shook the long staff he carried, and called out, "Why are you singing, Neckan? You should weep and mourn, for though you may live a thousand years, yet at the end you will die, and there's no salvation for you! Into the dark you will go, and you will be forgotten!"

The Neckan broke off its music and looked at the preacher a moment; then it exclaimed in a voice of pain and sorrow, "No salvation?"

"None!" cried the preacher. "Why, this staff I hold in my hand, withered and dead as it is, will bud and leaf before the day you shall be redeemed!"

The Neckan gave a long cry, and threw its harp into the deep pool, where it sank with one, deep, water-drawn chord; and the Neckan cried out a second time, and threw itself from the rock after the harp, and disappeared beneath the water.

The preacher climbed on up the mountain track, no longer angry, but full of the sense of strength and goodness that comes from bringing a creature of darkness to knowledge of its doom. He smiled as he climbed, and turned his bearded face to catch the breeze; he looked with approval on the flowers God had created, and stooped to sniff their perfume. Pausing now and again, he took deep breaths of the air, and was contented. But, presently, he began to be bothered by a buzzing in his ears, and no matter how he turned his head, it would not go away. Bees circled round his head, and he was afraid of being stung, but though he waved his hand at them, they returned in greater and greater numbers. Then, glancing at his staff, he saw why. Not only had it budded and leafed, but it had budded and flowered, and from its sprays of deep blue flowers came a heavy and beautiful scent.

The preacher stood still on the mountainside, watching the bees struggle into the flowers, and wondering at the miracle; but when he remembered his words to the Neckan, he was ashamed, and he turned and climbed back down the mountain to the pool. There was the Neckan, waist-deep in its pool, and still weeping, its face hidden in its hands.

"Neckan," said the preacher, gently, from the bank. "Look." And, when the Neckan raised its head, the preacher held out the blossoming staff. The Neckan looked, and then, quick as a fish, dived beneath the surface of the pool, and rose again with its golden harp. It began to play, and to sing a song about the flowers and leaves which could grow even from a dead staff. The preacher sat on the bank, and listened, and admired his miraculous staff and the bees which came to visit it.

St. Cullen and the
Elves

ST. CULLEN did not like the company of others, for their behaviour distracted him from his thoughts on the goodness of God; so he searched for a lonely place, far from houses and paths, where he could make himself a hermitage, and he found such a place at the foot of Glastonbury Tor. There he built himself a small hut of branches and clay, and there he settled to live in silence and solitude.

But he had not been living there very long when, to his annoyance, two men came by and stopped to rest beside his door, without noticing his hut because, being built of stones and branches, clay and turf, it looked like nothing more than a small mound. They began to talk and St. Cullen, inside his hut, could not help but overhear what they said. One of the men told the other that the King of the Fairies had his palace on the top of the Tor, and he went on to describe the lovely ornaments, paintings and hangings to be found in that palace; the beautiful music to be heard there; and the food and clothes of the fairies, which were far better than anything to be found among mortals. St. Cullen had been kneeling quietly in his hut, waiting for the men to go away, but they went on and on talking about the fairies until the Saint was too angry to be quiet any longer, and he put his head out of his hut, and shouted, "Go away! Or if you will not do that, then be quiet, for I cannot bear to hear any more of this talk about devils."

The two men jumped to their feet and looked about everywhere before they saw the Saint's head poking out of what they had taken for a mound. Then one said, "We were not talking of devils, and the King of the Fairies will be insulted that you call him by such a name."

"The creatures you spoke of are not God's, and therefore they are devils," said the Saint. "Go away! Don't argue with me; I am a Saint."

The two men began to gather up their belongings and to move away, but one said, as they went, "You'll be sorry for what you have said, Saint. The King of the Fairies will certainly send for you."

But the Saint did not think so, and was happy enough to be rid of the two men. The next day, however, in the evening, a stranger, a small dark man, came to the Saint's cell, and asked if he would accompany him to the palace on the hill-top, where the King was waiting to receive him. St. Cullen looked up at the hill, but could see no palace, and he refused to leave his hut. The stranger said politely that, in that case, he would trouble him no more that day, but would return the following night; and then he went away.

Early the next evening, the stranger returned, and begged St. Cullen to go with him to the King's palace, for the King was very anxious to meet the Saint.

"Where is this palace?" Saint Cullen asked.

"There," said the stranger, and pointed. The Saint stepped out of his cell and looked up at the hill-top, but could see no building of any kind, either large or small; and so he went back into his hut, saying that he would not leave it.

"Then I will trouble you no further tonight," said the stranger, "but I shall come back tomorrow, and the next night, and the next, until you agree, for my King is determined to meet you."

When the stranger had gone away, St. Cullen left his cell, filled a bottle with stream water, and blessed it to make it holy. The next evening, when the stranger returned, the Saint agreed to go with him, but hid his bottle of holy water under his cloak.

He climbed the hill with the small, dark man, but not until they had almost reached the top did he see the palace. It was full of light, and seemed to have a great many windows and doors; and the sound of music, and the scent of food and drink drifted to the Saint on the air.

The Saint and his companion reached the palace, and entered into a room of dazzling light and dizzying music. Round the walls hung tapestries in rich, bright colours, and in the centre of the room was a table loaded with food: hot meats sizzling in their grease, hot cakes and fruit and wine. The smell almost overpowered the Saint, who was not used to seeing or eating such large amounts of food. The elves crowded close about him, to see and touch him, and the light flashed from their jewels and golden chains and ornaments, and from their black eyes, as sunlight flashes from a mirror—and then the crowd parted to allow the Fairy King, wearing his golden circlet, and attended by many little pages, all dressed in red and blue livery, to approach the Saint. "You are very welcome, Cullen," said the King. "I have waited a long time to meet you. I hear that you consider us devils, but, tell me, have you ever heard of such splendour as this amongst the miseries of Hell?"

Cullen looked about at the fairy palace. "I think little of a hillside cave, muddy, filthy, and running with water," he said, and, at once, the glamour was destroyed, and the wet and dirty walls began to show through the hangings, and the smell of wet earth to smother the smell of food.

The King quickly led the Saint to the table, hoping to distract him, and invited him to eat as much as he liked, so that they might be friends, since they were already neighbours. But St. Cullen looked at the food with disgust, and said, "I do not eat the dried and shrivelled leaves from a tree"; and at once the hot meats and cakes and fruits were seen for what they really were.

But the elves could not believe that the Saint could see through their glamour, and the King said to him, "How do you like my pages? Do I not have more than any other king? Is not their livery of scarlet and blue fine?"

"It is apt," said the Saint. "Blue for the eternal cold, and red for the eternal flames, of Hell; and Hell is your proper place." And he took the bottle of holy water from beneath his cloak, and threw it over them all. The last of the music stopped on the instant, leaving only a dull silence. The walls, the tables, the courtiers, all disappeared, and there was not even a cave. St. Cullen stood in the cold air on the open hillside, with grass beneath his feet and a dark sky over his head.

He climbed back down the hill and went into his cell; prayed, and went to bed.

The elves were never seen in that country again.

The Bogey

THERE was once a bogey who haunted a river pool, and although he was rarely seen while it was still light, few people would go near that pool by night or day. It was known as the Old Bogey Hole, and it belonged to a rich farmer, who owned a great deal of the land in that part of the country. The bogey used to work for the farmer in return for milk and bread, which was left for him on the farmhouse doorstep at night. The bogey kept the yards, barns, byres and stables tidy, and was a good hand at mowing, stooking and threshing in season, so he earned his keep, and the farmer was careful to do nothing that might offend him.

The farmer's daughter saw the bogey often, and, since she had been taught since childhood to think of him as a friend, she was one of the few people who were not afraid of him, and she would often walk by the Old Bogey Hole, and no harm ever came to her. It began to be said that she was under the bogey's protection, and this view was strengthened when, the night after it became known that the girl was to be married, a bale of white silk was thrown at the farmhouse door and fell on the step. Who but the bogey could have provided it? The girl's wedding dress was made from the silk, and the bogey was not forgotten on her wedding night, his bowl being filled with ale instead of milk, and his bread replaced with cake. All that night he was heard singing drunkenly about the farm in the darkness.

The new husband came to live in his wife's house, and helped his father-in-law with the farm-work; and within a year gossip said that the new wife was expecting a child; and then the months went by until it was time for her to have it. It was in the Autumn, and the young woman's first labour pains began in the middle of a particularly stormy night. Her husband ran out into the yard to wake the stable-lad, and ordered him to ride as fast as he could to fetch the midwife, while the girl's mother and father shouted from their bedroom window that the boy was to ride by the quickest way.

The stable-lad began to dress, but very slowly. He wished no harm to his master's daughter, but he knew that the quickest way to the midwife was to ride straight through the Old Bogey Hole, and he was afraid, and was putting off the time that he must go near that haunted place as long as possible. But the bogey, going about his work in the yard, had heard the shouting and knew what was going on. He saw the stable-lad delaying, and guessed why. So he stole a cloak from behind the farmhouse door, mounted the best horse in the stables, and rode off to fetch the midwife at a faster pace than any human could have made the horse run.

He reached the midwife's house and hammered at her door and shutters, yelling out that she was needed and must come quick. She came hurrying out as soon as she could, and by that time the bogey was back on the horse and closely wrapped in his stolen cloak. The midwife took him for one of the men from the farm, and allowed him to help her up on to the horse, and clung tightly to him as they set off once more at a gallop. Though she thought it the hardest, swiftest gallop she had ever known (and she had been fetched in a hurry a few times) she wasn't worried until she realized that they were on the road which led to the Old Bogey Hole.

"Oh, don't go by the Old Bogey Hole," she said. "We might meet the bogey, and I'm scared."

"Never mind, old girl," said the horse's rider. "You've met all the bogeys you're going to meet tonight." And she was a little comforted.

They rushed through the pool, throwing up water on all sides, and were back at the farm in so short a time that the stable-lad was only just pulling on his boots. While the midwife hurried into the house, the bogey dragged the boy out into the yard and gave him a good hiding, saying, "That's for not taking better care of your mistress."

The farmer's daughter had a baby girl, and when he found out about the bogey's errand from the stable-lad, the farmer was almost as proud of his bogey as he was of his daughter and granddaughter. He told the story to everyone he met; he even told it to the priest, who said that such a good servant ought to be baptized. The farmer wasn't sure of this, but he didn't like to argue with the priest, and before the old man knew where he was, the priest had invited himself to stay at the farm.

He arrived with a large flask full of holy water,

and asked many questions about the bogey's comings and goings. Then he went out into the stable and waited. Some time after midnight, the bogey came into the stable to see if the place needed tidying, and the priest raised the flask of holy water high, and poured its contents all over him. The bogey shrieked in pain and anger, and flailed his arms hopelessly to rid himself of the scalding waterdrops. He ran out into the yard, the priest running after him, but the bogey vanished in the darkness and only his angry cries could be heard.

The bogey never did any more work for the farmer, nor was he seen for many years after that, and some people said that the priest's holy water had sent him to Hell, while others thought that he had only gone away to another part of the country. Most people, though, were still afraid to go near the Old Bogey Hole, and in this they were right, for the bogey was still there. It was the farmer himself who saw the very last of the bogey, and it happened as he was leading his plough-team home, late one spring evening. He was passing the pool when the bogey suddenly jumped up in his way, and said, "Give us a lend of your horses, man."

The farmer was very startled, and it took him a moment to catch his breath; and then he thought that he didn't want to lend his horses to a creature that wasn't even human. "My horses?" he said. "What do you want my horses for?"

"I need 'em," said the bogey. "Since they built that new church just down the hill there, my old woman, and my childer, and me, we can't get any rest for them blasted ding-dongs they strung up in the tower. So lend us your horses, man, to help us move out of hearing of 'em; I always helped you before."

The farmer had to admit that this was true, and he handed over the leading reins of his horses to the bogey, and went on home without looking back. He spent an anxious evening and night waiting for his horses' return, but when they did trot down into the yard the next morning, they had glossier coats and a more dancing step than he'd seen in them for years. They looked like two-year-olds, and worked like them, so the bogey more than paid for the loan of them. But where the bogey had moved his family, with the help of the farmer's horses, was never discovered. It must have been well out of earshot of the new church's bells, since he was never again seen in that district, and people even stopped speaking of his old pool as haunted.

King Olaf's Warning

ONE OF the first Christian kings of Norway was Olaf Tryggvason. He was feared because of his powers of foresight and the magical protection which his new faith gave him, and because of his attempts to convert his countrymen to Christianity by killing or maiming them if they would not leave the worship of their old gods.

So the King's words were attended to when he announced, one evening, that he had been sent a vision, and the vision had told him that it would be most dangerous for any man to go outside alone that night, and so, if any man wished to visit the privy, he must waken a friend to go with him. All the servants and soldiers who slept in the King's hall promised to do this.

Much later, when everyone had been asleep for hours, a man named Thorstein, who had eaten and drunk too much before lying down, woke in great discomfort, with a strong need to go to the privy. As he got hastily to his feet, he remembered the King's warning, and so he tried to wake a friend who was sleeping near him; but it was as if some spell of dullness lay over the sleepers in the hall, and though they muttered and turned, they would none of them wake—and Thorstein could not waste very long in trying to wake them, for his need grew more and more urgent until, at last, he had to ignore the King's warning, and dash out of the hall as quickly as he could.

The Royal Privy was a magnificent building, with strong walls and a high roof, and inside, eleven seats along each of the longer walls, so that twenty-two of the courtiers or garrison could ease themselves at once, in comfort and good company. Thorstein hurried in, unfastening his trousers, and dropped himself down over the hole nearest to the door, so that he could run back to the hall the quicker; but as he sat there he suddenly felt, on that side of him furthest from the door, a cold draught, and then a breath of heat. A stink of sulphur, and of ashes, crept to his nostrils, and all the hairs of his head, beard and body began to stir. He looked out of the corners of his eyes, and he thought he saw something move; so he fractionally turned his head—and then he cried out in terror as he saw, rising from the furthest privy, a creature more hideous than his own nightmares or any artist's carving had ever shown him.

The creature rose completely from the privy and appeared to sit on it, and it looked at Thorstein. There were nine empty seats between them. "It's a good night, Thorstein," the creature said.

In fear and horror, Thorstein cried out, "What are you?"

"I am one of those old heroes, Thorstein, who, in ancient times, fought with the great Harald Wartooth of Denmark. You will have heard tell of us, surely?"

"But Harald Wartooth is long dead," Thorstein said. "How are you come here?"

"I am long dead too," said the creature, "and I am come up from Hell. In my day we had not heard of your King's Christ, and we are all damned."

"Come up from Hell?" cried Thorstein. "Why? Why have you come?"

Then the creature gaped and grinned, and said, "For you, Thorstein."

Thorstein tried to jump up from his seat, to run back to the safety of the hall, but found that he was fixed in his place, for the same spell of dullness and weakness gripped him as had formerly prevented him from waking his friends. He looked again at the thing, and saw it preparing to move towards him, and he knew then that he would have to talk, and talk, for his life and for his soul.

"You come from Hell," he called out. "Then tell me——I have often wondered——of all the damned, who bears the pains of Hell most bravely and with least outcry?"

The creature sank back on to its seat. "That would be Sigurd, the Volsung, who slew the dragon and bathed in its blood."

"And what torture does he endure?" Thorstein asked hastily, as soon as it had finished speaking.

"He kindles an oven," said the creature.

"What? Kindles an oven? No wonder he bears it bravely. That is no very terrible torture."

"I do not think you would bear it so bravely, Thorstein," said the creature. "The kindling Sigurd uses is himself."

Thorstein was so astonished at this that he fell

silent and almost did not notice when the creature began to move again. But he recovered in time, and called out, "And who bears the pains of Hell least bravely, and with the most outcry?"

The creature sank back on to its seat again. "That would be Starkad the Old, even though, in life, he was among the most courageous of Odin's warriors."

"What is his torture?"

"He lies with his ankles in the fire."

"His ankles in the fire? And he one of Odin's most courageous warriors? Surely a truly brave man would bear that with more fortitude?"

"I do not think you would do so," said the creature. "His ankles are in the fire, but only the soles of his feet are out of it; and he yells, Thorstein. Would you like to hear how loudly he yells?"

Before Thorstein could reply, the thing opened its mouth and gave such a shriek that the sound struck Thorstein like a blow, and caused darkness to pass before his eyes as if he had blinked. With horrible speed, during that blink of darkness, the creature moved three seats closer to him, and said, "That is how Starkad yells when his pain is least. When it is greater, *this* is how he screams."

Thorstein tried again to speak, but before he

could, the creature screamed again, even more loudly and roughly. The sound tore at Thorstein's head, and the darkness came again, but for a longer time. When he could see once more, the thing was only three seats from him, grinning and gloating, and saying, "But this is how Starkad shrieks when his pain is at its worst."

Thorstein knew that this time he would lose his senses completely, and the thing would reach him, and carry him down to Hell; but as the thing screeched, and as Thorstein, still fixed to his seat, fell back in a dead faint, the bell of the King's chapel jangled, ringing loudly through the darkness and the murk of the demon's spell. With a groan, the demon sank down through the seat on which it was then sitting, and friends rushed into the privy to lift Thorstein up from the floor where he had fallen as the spell broke.

He was helped back to the hall, where the chapel bell was still ringing, and where the King was waiting to see if he had been saved; for it had been the King, uneasy about the vision he had received, who had risen in the night to see that all were safe, and, missing Thorstein from his sleeping-place, had ordered the bell to be rung immediately.

Thorstein was so grateful to the King for his

salvation that he became one of his most faithful followers, and so shaken was he by his terrible experience in the Royal Privy that it was said he became one of the most pious and devoted Christians to be found in the whole of Norway.

Merlin

THERE was once a boy whose mother was a nun, but whose father was a devil. As soon as the nun told of the devil's visit to her, priests were sent for, and they made the sign of the cross over her, and sprinkled her with holy water, and gave her holy water to drink, and because of these remedies, when the child was born, he seemed to be a normal human child. He was named Merlin, and, as soon as he could leave his mother, he was taken away to a monastery to be raised by the monks.

There he was taught to read and write, and proved a very clever boy, but no matter how the monks tried, they could not make him pious. He would not attend chapel, nor pray, nor cross himself, saying that all these things made him itch, and he showed other talents which the monks did not like, and which made them fear him; for Merlin could heal sickness and wounds, could read minds, and could foresee the future and look into the past. This, the monks said, was the result of the devil's blood in him, and many times they beat him to try to drive the devil out, but they could not make him a Christian, and while he was still a small boy, he ran away from the monastery.

For many years the monks heard nothing of him, and they worried often about what kind of creature they had let loose on the world; but then news reached them that, far to the north, where the people were still not Christians, the pagan King, Gwentholeu, had a new court poet, a man not only greatly skilled in the making of verses, but in healing and foretelling the future, and this poet's name was Merlin. He had won the favour of King Gwentholeu, although he was still a boy, and was dressed almost as finely as the King himself, with a golden ring, set with jewels, about his neck. A story was told of his most famous prohecy which filled the monks with both wonder and dread. Soon after Merlin had arrived at the court of King Gwentholeu, a newborn baby boy had been brought to him, and its parents had asked him to tell the child's fortune. Merlin had told them to prepare themselves for sorrow: the child would not live for long. The father had then asked him how the child would die. "By falling from a cliff," Merlin had replied. A little later, the child's uncle had come, and had asked Merlin how the child would die. "By hanging," Merlin had said, but when he was asked the same question a third time, his answer had been, "By drowning." Now people had begun to disbelieve in Merlin's powers of prophecy, for if he did not trust them himself, then how were others to trust them? But in little more than a year they were shown how accurate Merlin's prophecies could be: the child, then toddling, escaped from its mother one day, and found its way to a stream which ran in a deep gulley. It stumbled and fell over the gulley's edge, but its legs and long skirt became caught in a thorn bush, and there it hung, its head in the water. When found, it was dead.

Merlin grew to be a young man, no different in appearance from other young men, except that he was extraordinarily hairy. He remained the poet of King Gwentholeu, and was no less favoured by that King than when he had first come to his court; but while Merlin had been growing, Christianity had been spreading, and even the kingdom neighbouring that of Gwentholeu's had become Christian. This was the kingdom of Strathclyde, ruled by King Rytherch, who, since becoming a Christian, had been advised by a Christian holy man, a saint named Kentigern, who was very devout and eager to convert the whole country to his new faith. He began to urge King Rytherch to make war on the remaining pagan kingdoms, and force them to accept the Way and the Light, since they would not listen to peaceful preaching.

King Gwentholeu, and the rulers of the other pagan countries further north, began preparing their defence; and Merlin began to work on his king, as Kentigern was working on Rytherch. Do not merely defend, Merlin said; attack! Drive back these Christians. You have worshipped your gods since the beginning of your people; will you give them up now? Treat the Christians as they would treat you; make war on them, destroy them, drive them from our country; and your name will be remembered with love by all those who worship our gods in the centuries to come.

And, eventually, things fell out as both Merlin and Kentigern wished; a Christian and a Pagan army met, and a battle was fought. Kentigern urged his army to fight for the salvation of their souls, for new glory, for God's city on earth; Merlin urged his army to fight for the gods of their fathers, for ancient glory, for all their old and loved ways. Then both joined their armies, Kentigern in his grey robe, a club in his hand and a cross about his neck; Merlin in his brightly coloured clothes of expensive cloths, a golden ring about his neck, and a sword as his weapon. The battle was fought for a day, and, at the end, it was the Christians who won. Merlin's King, Gwentholeu, was killed; the pagans were chased from the field, and Merlin found himself among the corpses of men whom he had persuaded to fight a battle fated to be lost. He wept, and, as he wept, he heard a loud voice cry out, "Merlin, devil's child! See what slaughter you have caused! Your guilt is great and since you have chosen to give yourself to the Devil, and since your very nature is diabolical, you shall live with brutes until the day of your death." Merlin looked up and was dazzled by the enormous figure of a shining angel; he was terrified and ran away. He lost his wits and went into the forest, and wandered there for many years. His clothes were ripped from him by thorns, and he had only his natural hairiness to keep him warm in the winter; he lost the power of human speech, for he heard only the talk of birds and animals; and he lived on leaves and roots, berries, nuts, raw eggs, and raw meat, like any animal.

St. Kentigern, during this time, was travelling about the newly conquered pagan kingdoms, preaching the words of Christ. As he was walking one day, to a village where he was to preach, he saw a large, hairy creature, something like a man, watching him from the thick undergrowth beside the road. The Saint stopped and stared back at the thing, and saw that it *was* a man, but a naked, hairy, filthy and wild-looking man. The Saint held out his hands and spoke gently, and, after a long time, with much patience, persuaded the wild man to come to him. Then the Saint sat down with the stranger, and talked to him of Jesus Christ and Salvation. The wild man listened, and suddenly the power of speech returned to him, and he spoke his name—"Merlin" —and then went on, eagerly, to tell the Saint of how he had urged the pagans to fight against the Christians, and of how the Christians had won, and the Christian God had cursed him with madness and a life among the brutes.

"Do not despair," Kentigern said. "Our God is ever ready to forgive one who truly repents; he rejoices more over a sinner saved than over the salvation of righteous men. Repent, Merlin; come to Christ." But Merlin jumped up and ran away.

Then Kentigern knelt and prayed earnestly that God would lift the curse from Merlin, for in his present state he was little better than an animal, but once restored to human society, he might repent and come to Christ at last. Kentigern's prayer was answered, for soon afterwards Merlin came upon a spring of water where no water had been before. He drank from it, and was calmed, and his wits returned. He realized that he had been mad, and that he was naked, and he remembered his talk with the Christian holy man. He went at once to find Kentigern.

Kentigern was delighted to see him, and gave him food and clothes, and asked him if he now wished to become a Christian.

"I wish that I had not urged my King and his followers to fight against you," Merlin said, "because I see now that the coming of your new faith was fated; but for myself, I still think of the times when a man could worship what god he pleased."

"But they were unloving gods," said Kentigern. "Come now, Merlin; accept the body and the blood, and become a Christian."

But Merlin got to his feet and said, "I will no longer fight against you, for I see that it is no use, but neither will I break faith with my dead King and friends, with my gods and with my father. I will never accept your body and blood."

"I foresee a time when you will," said Kentigern.

"I doubt your powers of prophecy, Christian," Merlin said, "but now I will prophesy. I foresee that neither you, nor your King Rytherch, will live a day longer than I, for all the great power of your loving god."

Kentigern shook his head, and said, "This is the blood of the devil in you."

Merlin left Kentigern, and travelled the country as a poet and story-teller, often prophesying, and always remaining faithful to his old gods and his father. At last he came to the court of King Uther Pendragon, who admired Merlin's poetry so greatly that he gave him the position of Court Poet, despite the fact that he knew Merlin to be of demonic birth, and a pagan. In a very short while, Merlin became the King's most valued adviser, for even if his prophecies were devilish, they were useful. It was Merlin who foretold that King Uther would be killed shortly before the birth of his son, and that the baby's life would be in danger, but that if he survived, he would become the greatest and most famous King that had ever reigned, or ever would reign, in Britain; and it was Merlin who, after King Uther's death, smuggled the baby away to a place of safety; and it was Merlin who named him Arthur.

From that time Merlin worked to ensure that the boy would achieve the glorious reign he had foreseen for him. Merlin oversaw his education, devised a means for him to gain the throne, advised him after his accession, and provided him with his sword, Excalibur. He served the young King well and faithfully in everything, although Arthur, like his father, was a Christian. Merlin himself never ceased to mourn for the passing of the old faith, and it is said that after he had seen the pagans defeated in the last battle against the Christians, he laughed only three times more in his life. The first time was when he saw a husband and wife together, the husband tenderly patting his wife's hand, and the wife smiling at him with loving kindness. But Merlin saw leaves caught in their hair, and knew that they had both come straight to one another from a forest meeting with other lovers. The second time he laughed was when he saw a ragged, starving beggar sitting by the roadside, for Merlin saw that the man was sitting directly above a hoard of gold and silver packed into an alabaster vase. He laughed for the third time when he overheard a young man boasting of the new shoes he had just bought, which were so well made, and of such fine leather, that the shoemaker had assured him that they would last for seven years. Merlin knew that the young man would be killed the next day.

The end of Merlin's life on earth came when he fell in love with a beautiful lady of Arthur's court, the lady Vivienne. Although Merlin knew very well that she did not love him, he could not help but love her, and he followed her everywhere, until people began to sneer and laugh at him whenever Arthur could not hear them. Vivienne pretended to love Merlin in return, until she had learned what seemed to her the greater part of his magic; and then, as they sat beneath an oak tree one day, she caused the tree's trunk to open and enclose Merlin, so that he was a prisoner inside it, and then she went away. Three days after this, one of King Arthur's knights was riding by the tree when he heard Merlin calling out from within it. The knight dismounted and begged Merlin to tell him how he could break the spell, but Merlin replied that this was impossible. He wanted the knight to ride to Arthur's court and tell the young king what had happened, and warn him that, in the future, he would no longer be able to rely on his adviser's guidance. Then the knight heard Merlin call out to his father, asking for help and rescue, and, although it was mid-day, the sun was suddenly covered, and everything became as black as midnight. In the darkness, the terrified knight heard a rushing sound, and a rising gabble of unearthly voices. Merlin gave one last shout, which was heard three miles away, and at that moment, far away at Arthur's court in Camelot, the candles in the chapel were all blown out, and the curtain behind Arthur's throne was ripped from top to bottom.

Then the sky cleared and daylight returned, and the knight saw that the oak tree had been split, as if by lightning. Of Merlin there was no trace, nor has he ever been seen since.

The Knight's Servant

THERE was once a knight who lived in a castle high above an important road, along which anyone in that part of the country who wished to visit friends or relatives; all people who wished to sell goods at market; and all merchants who wished to trade in the towns on the other side of the mountains, had to travel. The knight watched their comings and goings from his castle, and, whenever he saw a particularly rich party of travellers, he sent his men-at-arms down to the road to rob them. Some of the travellers thought to save their lives and property by fighting; but the knight's men always defeated them, because they had had more practice. Other travellers thought that if they gave up everything they had, they would be allowed to live, but they too were mistaken, for the knight had given orders that not a single person was to be allowed to escape. Soon, anyone still brave enough to travel by that road had to pass the wrecks of carts, discarded weapons, torn clothing, skeletons, and even more horrible sights.

But although the knight was so cruel, strangely, he had a great love of the Virgin Mary. The chapel of his castle was dedicated to Her, and every morning, and every evening, and at midday, he knelt before the painting of Her which hung above the altar, and asked Her to intervene for him with her Son. As a child he had been taught to pray to Her in this way, and he had never forgotten. There was never a morning when he was so hungry that he did not go to the chapel first; and never an evening when he was so tired that he went to his bed before kneeling to pray.

It happened that, one day, news was brought to the knight that a party of travellers had been sighted from the castle's tower. It was a large party, with many horses, and some important and, no doubt, rich person being carried in a litter. Even from the watch-towers necklaces, brooches and belts could be seen shining, and the knight very quickly decided that here was a party worth robbing, and sent his men down to attend to the business.

All those men who were ready armed ran and jumped down the dangerous path from the castle to the road, and set about the party of travellers with such speed and brutality that, in a few minutes, every one of them was killed——except the occupant of the litter. But when the curtains of the litter were ripped down, it was found that a Bishop had been sitting behind them, dressed in all his robes, and with a crucifix round his neck. At this the men drew back, being unwilling to kill a man of God in cold blood. Instead they began to gather up the weapons and purses of those they had killed. The Bishop left his litter and came among them, asking them to take him with them back to the castle, and to bring him before the knight who owned it. The men would not listen to him; they were afraid. Their arms full of stolen goods, they began their climb back to the castle's gates. The Bishop, though he was old and weak, hoicked up his holy robes, and followed them. He followed them right into the castle, and then began demanding that he should be taken to the knight.

No one wanted to be the one to tell the knight that the Bishop had been allowed to live and was inside his castle; but the Bishop began cursing them in the name of God, and insisting that they must take him to see the knight, because he had an important message to give him. Then the servants and men-at-arms were afraid, and they took the Bishop to the hall of the castle, where the knight was sitting.

"Are you the master of this castle," asked the Bishop, "the man who has caused the death of so many innocents, and who has defied the commandments, 'Thou shalt not steal,' and 'Thou shalt not kill'?"

The knight only grunted at this, and said, "What are you doing here, old man? Who let you in?"

"I am here to give you a message from the only person you are ever likely to listen to—the Sainted Virgin Herself," said the Bishop. "But before I tell you what it is, you must have all your servants called here so that I may see them."

"What are my servants to you?" asked the knight.

"It is the Virgin's wish," said the Bishop.

The knight was angered by this, but he would not deny a wish of the Virgin's and he sent for all his servants, telling them to come up to the castle's great hall. They came, and, as each of them entered, the Bishop called them to him, and blessed them. Last of all, and very reluctantly, came the knight's personal servant, a small, stooping man who helped the knight to dress every morning, and to undress every evening, and brushed his clothes and polished his boots. This small servant approached the Bishop a step at a time, slowly and more slowly, until he stopped altogether, at some distance from the holy man. The Bishop stretched out his hand to draw him closer but, to everyone's surprise, the little man began to twitch and squint. He began to chatter, and to pull faces; he twisted his body, and cringed down to the floor. He jumped up again, and arched over backwards until his head touched the floor behind him. He rolled himself up like a ball, he spun like a top, he bared all his teeth and opened wide his eyes. It was horrible to watch, and it went on until the Bishop said, "You pitiable creature—unable to stand before a man of God. Now, in the name of the Holy Trinity, go back to your true place."

Then, with a groan, and sinking like a punctured balloon, the servant sank through the floor.

The knight, who watched all this with horror and astonishment, turned to the Bishop with his mouth open.

"You have been most cruel and wicked all your life," the Bishop said to him, "and you have never repented of your misdeeds. This creature, that you saw just now, was placed in your household by the

Devil himself, that no time might be lost in carrying you to Hell. One thing, and one thing only, has been your salvation all these years, and that has been your devotion to Our Lady, the Ever-Virgin. She has guarded you from harm, so that you might have a chance to repent; but I tell you, in Her name, that if you had even once forgotten the prayers you make to Her, in the mornings, the evenings, and at midday, then that imp would have seized you with tooth and claw and snatched you away from your life. And now that you know how close you have been to damnation, I beg you, confess and repent. Return to the Church."

Then the robber knight knelt and put his hands between those of the Bishop, and confessed his sins, and repented; and he swore to give up his wicked life of robbery and murder.

From that day, the road which ran below the castle was safe for all travellers, for the knight never broke his vow. Indeed, to atone for all the sins he had committed, he went on a crusade to the Holy Land, where, with the Church's blessing, he destroyed many of the heathen, and brought back so much of their wealth that he was able to present the Bishop with a statue of the Virgin made of pure gold.

The Soldier and the
Changeling

T HERE was a soldier who was returning home
after many years of fighting abroad. His skin
was burnt to a dark brown, his hair was long and
uncombed, and there hung round his waist, and
banged his leg, a heavy, clumsy sword. A bundle of
belongings was fastened to his back, and he hugged
about himself an old cloak which was worn so thin
that in places the colour of his shirt could be seen
through it.

He had been travelling all day, and it was growing
very dark, but the soldier trudged on. He was near
home, and thought that he might as well sleep under

his own roof, and save the price of lodgings; but the way was longer than he had reckoned, and when it was almost midnight, he was still walking. This is how he came to overhear the witches talking. He was on one side of the hedge, and they were on the other, and he heard one of them say, "A good morning to you, sister. Has it been a good night?"

"A good night, sister, a good night," replied the other. "I flew to the coast on the back of the miller's son—him being in the shape of a horse —and there I threw six cats, all tied together, into the sea, and so raised a storm that will not be forgotten for a hundred years. But tell me, sister, has it been a good night for you?"

"It has been a good night, a good night indeed," said the first witch. "See what I have here." The soldier, listening, heard the witches exclaim with pleasure, and wondered what it was they had, and he crept closer to the hedge to try to see; but it was much too dark. Then one of the witches said, "Whose child is it?"

"Ah; that would be telling, sister; but it is a child that will be much missed, I promise you."

"And what did you leave in its place?" asked the other witch.

"One of the elves' children from under the hill:

an ugly, screeching, nasty little thing. It will make the parents screech!"

The witches began to laugh; but the soldier now knew that they had a human baby which they were going to give to the elves, and he knew that the elves would pay their tax to Hell with it, while the changeling had the best of everything and plagued the life out of the poor couple who believed it to be their child. The soldier drew his sword, knowing that its cold iron would protect him, and he pushed right through the hedge, saying, "In the name of Jesus Christ, give up that child!"

The witches were so alarmed that they at once changed themselves into hares and sped away. The soldier caught the baby as it fell from where the witch's arms had been, and he used his cloak for wrapping the child, since, after pushing through the hedge, there was hardly enough left to wrap round himself. After that he went on to his home, and woke his mother and his brothers and sisters by banging at the door. They were all astonished to see him, because for many years they had not known whether he were alive or dead; and they were even more astonished to see him carrying a baby in his arms; but when they had quietened down, he told them how he had rescued the child from the witches.

"Look after the baby, Mother," he said, giving it to her, "and very soon we shall hear who it belongs to, and we'll be able to give it back."

Then, although his family wanted to start celebrating, the soldier went to bed. He was very tired.

Daylight came, and, with it, a piece of gossip which was carried from door to door, and eventually to the soldier's mother. Had she heard about all the fuss up at the big house? Did she know that the lord's little son had been stolen? The lord's son! Stolen away in the night, and the nastiest, ugliest thing you couldn't wish to meet left in its place.

"Well, well, fancy that," said the soldier's mother, and went inside straight away to wake her son. As soon as he heard, he said, "The lord's son, eh? If it had been anyone else, I should have given them back the child, and have been glad to do it; but since it's the lord, he can afford to pay me a little for all the trouble I had in the wars."

Then he got up, wrapped the baby in his ragged old cloak so that it was quite hidden, walked over to the lord's house, and knocked at the door. When the lord answered, and asked what he wanted, the soldier replied, "I am a famous wizard, and I have come to restore your son to you."

When the lord heard this, he immediately asked the soldier in, and led him up to the nursery, where the lord's wife was standing over the cradle, looking pale and frightened. "Don't worry any more," the soldier said to her. "I am a wizard, and I shall soon have your son back." He then went close to the cradle, and looked inside, and saw a creature no bigger than a baby, but with the appearance of a tiny, shrivelled old man. It blinked at the soldier and curved its mouth up in a thin, sly smile. The soldier turned to the lord and lady. "I shall need an egg, a dish, a small spoon, a jug of water, a towel, and some malt," he said, "and the quicker I am given these things, the sooner you will see your son again."

The lord sent a servant running to fetch these things, and, while they were waiting, the lady said to the soldier, "Can you really bring back our son?"

"If you can," said the lord, "I will give you anything you ask for—anything—land, money, cattle—"

"We'll talk about that later," said the soldier. "But I shall ask for the price my skill deserves, you can be sure of that."

Just after he said this, the servant returned with the things he had asked for, and putting his bundle down carefully in the corner, the soldier began to perform his spell. First, he moved the nursery table closer to the cradle, so that the creature inside it could see what he was doing. Then he broke the egg into the dish, washed out one half of the broken shell, and dried his hands, one finger at a time. The creature in the cradle took hold of the cradle's edge with one bony hand, and raised itself slightly, to have a better look at what he was doing. The soldier pretended not to notice, but poured water from the jug into the eggshell, until it was almost full. The creature in the cradle was seen to raise its eyebrows, but again the soldier pretended not to have noticed anything. He took up the little spoon, and spooned a tiny quantity of malt into the eggshell, and, with the creature in the cradle watching him fixedly, he took the shell to the fire, and began to heat it at the edge of the embers.

"I can no longer keep quiet," said the creature in the cradle. "What are you doing, man?"

"Isn't it plain what I'm doing?" asked the soldier. "I'm brewing ale."

There was a pause, and then the creature said, "I am old, ever so old; I have seen three forests grow and wither; I have seen the seas run dry and fill; but I have never in all my long, long years seen a soldier brew his ale in an eggshell before."

"Aah!" the soldier cried, swinging round on it. "You ancient, ugly, wicked thing! You have given yourself away; now in the name of God the Father, Christ the Son, and the Holy Ghost, be gone!"

He made a grab at it, as if he would remove it by force, but, quicker than a snake, the thing was out of the cradle, and across the room; and with a hiss and a crackle, a flash of green flame, a hot, ashy smell, and a loud shriek, it vanished up the chimney.

There was a great sigh from the lady, the lord, and all the others in the room, but the soldier turned to them, and said, "Now you must all leave, while I perform the most secret spells for the return of your child. Go, please, quickly, and no matter what noise you hear, or how long the silence may last, do not come in. If you come in before the struggle is over, both the child and I will be snatched away by dark powers." He shooed them all to the door, and repeated, as he closed the door on them, "Whatever you hear, or do not hear, do not come in."

As soon as the door was closed, the soldier took up his cloak, unwrapped the child hidden in it, and placed the baby in the cradle. Then he began to bang on the table with his hands, and to shout and stamp; he whistled and dragged chairs about the room, clapped his hands and chanted magical-sounding words. Then he stood absolutely still, hugging himself and grinning, and keeping quiet; he kept quiet for so long that the people waiting anxiously outside the door began to sigh and and moan, and to put their hands on the latch. Then the soldier shouted so loudly that he terrified them; he shouted and clattered the furniture and slammed cupboard doors and rattled the window-frames; and then he went and opened the door. He drooped as he did so, and mopped his brow, and looked exhausted. "It was a hard struggle," he said, "but I won."

He was almost knocked from his feet by the people rushing into the room. They all gathered round the cradle, and the mother lifted the child into the air, and turned to smile at the soldier.

"Name your reward!" said the lord. "What do you want?"

"A castle," said the soldier, "its treasuries filled with gold plate and coins, and precious stones. Round it, a good forty square miles of farmland—an orchard—a carp-pond—and stock and servants, of course."

"Ah," said the lord, turning a little pale. "Well—"

"Or, if that's too much," said the soldier, "I'll manage without the castle. Just provide me with the treasury, and the land, and I'll build my own."

"*Actually*——" said the lord.

"Perhaps all that would be too much to manage for me, with my war-wounds," said the soldier. "No, a small house will do—about the size of this one—with the forty square miles, the orchard, the carp-pond, the stock and the servants."

"A house," said the lord. "But forty miles . . ."

"A bit much for me to farm, I agree," said the soldier. "Say twenty square miles, then—and forget the carp-pond. I never liked fish."

"An orchard," said the lord. "Seven acres, and a little house."

"Throw in the stock and it's a deal," said the soldier.

"Done," said the lord, and the soldier went happily home to his mother and brothers and sisters, having gained a far greater reward than the one he'd been hoping for.

Blessing the Cliffs

IN ICELAND, along the fjords, there are steep cliffs where hundreds of seabirds build their nests, on ledges, and in little clefts in the rock; and they fly and scream over the cliffs and the sea.

The people of Iceland used to lower themselves over the edges of these cliffs on ropes, to steal the eggs from the birds' nests—but there were trolls living in the cliffs as well as birds, and too often a huge, grey hand, hung with shaggy fur, would come out of the cliff's side and tweak the ropes in two as if they were threads of cotton; and whoever was on the end of the rope fell, and was killed.

This habit of the trolls' grew so bad that the people asked a Bishop to come and pray over the cliffs, and exorcise the evil, heathen things that lived in them. The Bishop came in his heavy, brilliant, beautiful robes; and, attended by others as stiffly and magnificently dressed as himself, swinging censors and carrying candles, he paced slowly along the cliffs' edge, praying and sprinkling holy water, and calling upon the trolls to leave.

It took a long time, but, at last, only one small part of the cliffs was still unblessed. Before the Bishop could reach it, a deep, thick, unhappy voice cried out, "Bishop! Bishop! The wicked do need somewhere to live."

The Bishop stopped short in astonishment; but then he said, "That is so." And he left that part of the cliffs unblessed, and the trolls still live there. That is why it is called Heathen Cliff, and why no one goes near it.

Dando and his Dogs

ONCE, in Cornwall, there lived a priest named Dando. He was not a good man. He was arrogant and selfish. He thought that merely being a priest had saved his soul, and that he had no reason to fear God. He drank, he smoked, he swore; and he neglected his parish, never visiting any of his congregation except those that had pretty daughters or young wives, and preaching only when the day seemed to promise poor hunting. He thought he had done more than enough if, in crumpled vestments pulled on hurriedly, he performed a marriage-service, or christened a child; and he had been known to refuse to leave his house to administer the last rites because it was raining.

The one thing which Dando was always ready to do was hunt. He led the hunt, and his congregation knew that if the Sunday were fine, there was no point in going to church, for Dando would be out with his dogs. "Dando," said an old woman to him as he rode home on Sunday evening with his kills hung from his saddle, "if you hunt on a Sabbath, you will be hunted."

But Dando did not care for the opinion of an ignorant old woman who could not write her own name, and the next Sunday he went hunting again, on the estate called Earth. They had a long, hard chase and made several kills—for Dando would run down any animal that showed itself. Once or twice during the day he thought he noticed a stranger riding with the hunt: a dark, quiet-faced man; but when he looked again he always found that he had been mistaken, and it was some man he knew very well.

Late in the afternoon the hunt stopped beside a stream to rest the horses, and to eat and drink themselves. Dando put his flask to his mouth, and found that it was empty; he had drunk all the whisky it had held in pauses during the chase. Immediately he turned to the rider nearest him and demanded a drink from his flask. "It's empty too," the man said.

Dando turned to the rider on his other side, but that man's flask was also empty. Dando was angry then, and shouted out that anyone who had any drink left was to bring it to him. But every member of the hunt had emptied their flasks.

"Then get more!" Dando yelled.

"But, Dando, where shall we get it?" asked one of the huntsmen. "There is nowhere for miles where we can get drink."

"Well, if none can be found on Earth—go to Hell for it!" Dando shouted.

At that moment a horse was nudged close to Dando's, and on its back sat the dark, quiet-faced man whom Dando had fancied he'd seen several times that morning; but now Dando saw him plainly and, strangely, a coldness of fear came over him. His flesh shuddered, and his chitterlings seemed to creep within him. The man held out a flask to him and, over the flask, looked intently at Dando with bright eyes, green as new grass, which seemed, somehow, to be lit from within the man's skull.

"What's this?" Dando asked rudely, nodding at the flask; but his voice shook.

"It is the finest drink 'stilled in the place you just mentioned," said the stranger.

Every other member of the hunt sat motionless and without speaking, but Dando managed to laugh. "You won't frighten me with such talk, sir!" he said. "I want drink, and if it *does* come from Hell, I'll take it."

And he took the flask from the stranger's hand,

put it to his mouth, and took a gulp to show that he wasn't afraid. The drink was the best he'd ever tasted; and he took another drink, and another; and emptied the flask. Then he looked round boastfully, and blearily, for the drink had been strong, and he saw the dark, quiet man going from one member of the hunt to another, gathering together all the game and hanging it from his saddle. No one seemed to have the courage to deny him.

Then the stranger brought his horse close to Dando's again and, before Dando could say anything, took Dando's share of the kill, and added it to the game already hanging from his black saddle.

"What right have you?" Dando demanded, reddening, as he leaned from his saddle and tried to snatch his kills back.

"I have the right," said the stranger. "This is the Sabbath; your kills are my due."

"Your due, damn it!" shouted Dando. "Return it at once, sir, or I'll see you in Hell!"

The stranger smiled, but shook his head, and said, "What I have, I hold."

"Will you, by God, will you?" said Dando, and he tumbled clumsily from his horse, and rushed at the stranger, shouting, "I'll have it back if I have to follow you to Hell for it!"

The stranger laughed out loud—very loud—at that, and, seizing Dando by the scruff of his jacket, he lifted him from the ground and flung him across his saddle-bow as if he too were a kill. "What I have, I hold!" the stranger shouted again, and his black horse leaped forward, so fast and high that it might have been winged. It leaped straight into the middle of the stream, but, instead of water being flung up, there spurted into the air a rush of flame. When it died down, leaving the water bubbling, Dando and the dark stranger were gone.

Dando never hunted on the estate of Earth in life again, but someone did. Someone hunted there at night, in the deepest, unlit darkness; riding hard and headlong over the rough ground, passing through hedges and woodlands as if they were air; hunting with a pack whose savage and continual baying held those who heard it paralysed with fear until the sound had died away; and then left them despairing. No mortal could ride so recklessly in such darkness; no mortal ever owned such unearthly hounds, and so it was said that Dando's ghost now led the hunt—but one or two people who had heard those hounds could not believe that Dando was riding behind them. No, they said; he runs before.

The Troll Bride

Once, in Denmark, there was a young man who married a troll's daughter, a fine, strapping girl, much taller than he was, with tremendous shoulders and forearms, a head of golden hair stiffer than gold wire, and a long, strong tail which she wagged when she saw him. They married because they each felt perfectly suited to the other, and they were very happy together; but the people of the young man's village were not pleased at all. "What sort of marriage-service was that?" they said. " 'Do you take this man?—Do you take this troll?' That can't be right."

"Did you see how much the thing ate after the service?" others said. "Give it a week or two, and it'll be eating *him*."

Most often the villagers said, "What *can* he see in it?"

They were so suspicious of the troll bride that none of them would have anything to do with her, even though she tried hard to be friendly. The village children, who had been told that she would eat them, threw stones after her, called her names, and then ran from her in a panic; the women she spoke to turned their backs on her; and the men shied away from her as they might from a bear. They made her very unhappy; and even though her husband appealed to them to be kinder to her, they refused. "You wait," they told him, "until it shows its *real* nature." He went angrily back to his troll bride then, swearing that he would have nothing more to do with his own people.

One Sunday, while the villagers were in church, the troll bride's father, a huge old troll with stiff black hair and a black beard, came to the barn where the newly-married couple were living until the husband could build a house large enough for his wife. The old troll had travelled down from the mountains to visit his daughter and find out if she was happy. When he heard how the villagers were treating her, he was angry. He scowled so that his brows covered his eyes; he showed his long teeth; he lashed his tail. To his daughter, he said, "Will you throw or catch?"

"Oh Father," she said. "You won't hurt the poor little things?"

"Will you throw or catch?" repeated the big old troll, his hair bristling.

"I'll catch, Father," she said.

"Then come along," said the troll, and he left the barn, his daughter and much smaller son-in-law following.

The troll led them up the hill to the churchyard, where they waited, and listened to the murmur of prayers and the singing of hymns from inside the church. The service ended, the people came out—and crowded back into the church at the sight of an even bigger, fiercer and more frightening troll than the one they were already plagued with.

"Go round to the other side of the building, daughter," said the troll, and, when she had, he beckoned to the people inside the church. Some of them went out to him, too afraid to do anything but obey; others were pushed out by the priest, who was afraid that the troll would destroy his church to reach them if he did not. The troll picked them up one by one, and threw them over the church roof. They howled as they rushed upward, and flapped their arms, trying to fly; but it was worse when they felt themselves beginning to fall. Then their shrieks and moans were so comical that some of the villagers still on the ground couldn't help giggling, until the troll picked them up.

On the other side of the church the troll's daughter caught them as they came tumbling towards her, set them safely on their feet, straightened their clothes, and patted their heads. When her father had thrown every one of them—except his son-in-law—over the roof, he came round the corner of the building and found them all standing, sitting or lying about his daughter's skirts, all shaking hard enough to shake off their clothes.

"If I ever again hear that you have made my daughter unhappy," said the troll, "we shall play this game once more; but on that day, she will throw, and *I* will catch. Do you understand me, people?"

All the villagers understood him very well, and as soon as the troll had gone back to the mountains, everyone in the village began calling on the troll bride, to give her eggs and cakes, and helpful hints; and everyone who met her wished her good morning and smiled; and the villagers soon discovered that, despite her fierce appearance, she was kind and gentle, and eager to please. They forgot everything unkind they had said about her when she arrived, and went about telling each other that they had thought from the first day that she was a 'lovely thing'. Before long the troll bride was gossiping with the neighbours every day, helping with embroidery and knitting in the evenings, and minding children. She was happier than she had ever been, but her husband, who hardly ever saw her any more, was somewhat bitter.

The Origin of the Elves

I N THE days when Jesus was on earth, there was a
woman living in the north who had a great many
children; so many that she was rather ashamed of
them, because she could never keep all of them
equally clean and tidy, or equally well-dressed and
fed. One day she heard from her neighbours that
Jesus was in the district, and was coming that way,
and would probably stop to talk with them. The
woman hurried home, called all her children
together, and began to wash them and comb their
hair, to put clean clothes on them, to darn holes and
sew buttons, and let down hems; to inspect ears and

necks and fingernails, to wipe noses and muddy knees, and to say, "Stand up straight! Take your hands out of your pockets! Use your handkerchief! Don't scuff your shoes! Don't fidget, don't pull faces, don't muss your hair!"

But no matter how hard she tried, the children that she wasn't washing and tidying at any one moment ran away to play, and fell over and made their knees muddy and bloody; tore their clothes; fell in puddles; tangled their hair in tree-branches; and made themselves, in a dozen different ways, as untidy and grubby as they had been before she had started. So, when the poor woman, all hot and cross and panicky, looked up and saw, through her window, Jesus coming up the path to her house, half her children were clean and neat, and the other half looked as if they had always run wild and had never had anyone to care for them. The woman was ashamed for Jesus to see them, in case he thought her a bad mother who did not try to look after her children, and to all those children who had made themselves grubby again, she said, "Go out behind the house, and hide, and don't let Him see you."

Off they went, thinking it a game, and the woman let Jesus in, and gave him some food and drink; and Jesus sat in her house, and ate, and drank, and looked at the children whom she had made to stand in a row in front of Him.

"These are beautiful children, woman," he said, "and much loved; but where are the others?"

"I have no others," she said.

"No others?" said Jesus. "I was sure you had others."

"Only these," she said, and smiled proudly at the row of neat, clean, well-dressed children in front of her.

Jesus looked at her quietly for a moment, as if waiting for her to call in her other children; then he shook his head and said, "Were you afraid of *my* judgement? Let those that are hidden remain hidden; for if they are not fit for me to see, they cannot be fit to be seen by anyone."

Then Jesus went away, and the woman hurried out behind her house to call in the children that were hiding; but although she called all day, they did not come. Thinking that they were playing a joke on her, she went to look for them. She found their footprints where it was muddy; she found grass trampled down where they had played, and fruit that they had picked dropped on the ground; but of them – nothing. At Christ's command they had become the Hidden People – the Huldrefolk – the

Elves; and if they are seen, it is only for a moment, and then uncertainly.

Their mother is still searching for them; and sometimes she comes where children are playing, and goes from child to child, peering into their faces; but then she wanders away, calling, for they are never her children.

"Isn't it Fun in the Dark?"

I T WAS always the custom when a corpse was laid out awaiting burial, for someone to sit beside the body with a candle burning, to keep watch. If the body was that of a close friend or relative, the duty of watching was considered an honour, and there were plenty of people willing to do it; but once, in Iceland, a man died who had no friends, and no relatives who cared to admit the relationship.

In life this man had been a powerful wizard, able to raise a thick fog by whirling a goat's skin round his head, call up the dead to question them, and create monsters by magic art which he could then cause to attack people. Nor had he ever been a Christian, but had boasted openly, without fear, of his worship of the wicked old gods, Odin, Thor and Freyr. His body had been washed and laid out, but no one dared to sit beside it through the three long nights of the watch, even with a candle—but neither did they dare to leave the body of such a wicked man unattended. So, as the time drew near for the watch to begin, and still no one had been found to undertake it, many of the neighbourhood went together to speak to a certain man who was known to be both strong and courageous, and they begged him to watch the wizard's corpse. The man liked the idea of the watch as little as his friends, but he understood that someone had to do it; and he had been asked; and so he agreed.

For the first two nights of the watch, nothing happened. The old wizard lay as still and quiet as a corpse should; the candle-flame rocked gently to and fro on the top of its tallow-column; and the watcher smoked his pipe, and hummed to himself, and gradually became easier in his mind until, at the beginning of the third night's watch, he told his neighbours that he was looking forward to the peace and quiet.

But that night, a little before dawn, the candle

went out; and in the sudden, smoky darkness, before the watcher could move to make another light, the dead wizard beside him slowly sat up, and said, "Isn't it fun in the dark?"

The watcher gasped in horror; but knew that he had to think and act quickly if he was to save his life. "Fun maybe," he said, "but not for you!" And then he grabbed the corpse by the shoulders and tried to force it down on to the table. The corpse fought him, and it was very strong; and he thought that the breath it cast in his face would make him faint; but they had not been struggling above a minute when the first real light of day shone through the window and on to the corpse's face. "Oh, thank God!" said the man, and whether it was the naming of God, or the daylight touching it, the corpse sank back upon the table and moved no more.

The wizard was buried that day, and a huge stone laid on his grave before nightfall to prevent him from getting up again.

Kraka

KRAKA was a troll, a giantess, who lived high in the mountains of Iceland, in a cave. She was very strong and fierce, and she used to steal cows by picking them up and walking off with them; and these cows she would eat raw, and crack their bones for the marrow. She used to eat people too, but only women and girls, never men, because she liked men. She thought they were pretty. She used to steal men, and carry them home to her cave and keep them; but they never stayed with her longer than they could help. Kraka never gave up hope that one would stay, though, and no young man with any looks was safe from her.

There was a farm not far from where Kraka lived, called Baldursheim, and on this farm there worked a shepherd called Jon. He was a handsome young man, and the farmer secretly wondered how long it would be before Kraka took him, but he said nothing, for Jon was an excellent shepherd, and he didn't want to frighten him away.

As for Jon himself, it never occurred to him that the giantess might notice him; never, until the day he looked round to find that she had crept up silently behind him. As soon as he saw her, before he could run, she swung him over her shoulder and carried him off to her cave.

Kraka's cave was hard to reach, and once set down on the cave's floor, Jon realized that he was going to find it far from easy to escape; and for a long time it was impossible because Kraka stayed in the cave with him. She crooned over him and stroked his hair, and called him by names which he found far from reassuring, such as 'Tidbit' and 'Sweet Morsel'. He sat looking at the bones which poked from the rubbish on the floor, and said nothing at all.

After a while Kraka wanted him to eat something; and she fetched him all the things which a Troll considers delicacies; but Jon, although he was hungry, wouldn't eat any of her food because he was afraid of what it might be; and because he who eats a troll's food becomes a troll himself.

After a day or two Jon began to look thin and ill, and Kraka became worried that her pet might die. She begged him to eat, and even tried to push food into his mouth; but he spat it all out. Eventually, when he saw that the monster was really concerned for him, he said, "There's only one thing I can think of that might tempt my appetite."

"What, what?" Kraka said.

"A twelve-year-old shark," he said.

Kraka was silent for a long time, as she knew that the only place where she could catch a twelve-year-old shark was off Siglunes, and that was a good seventy miles from her cave. But, after she had tried again to persuade him to eat and he still refused to swallow even the smallest crumb of bone-bread, she became desperate, and decided that she had better go and get the shark.

She told Jon several times that it would be best for him if he stayed where he was, and then she left the cave and started out for Siglunes. But she hadn't gone much further than twenty miles when she suddenly became sure that the shepherd had run away as soon as she had turned her back—and at once she ran back to the cave and peered in. Jon was sitting quietly in the corner where she had left him, with his hands folded in his lap.

She started out again, and this time covered, perhaps, twenty-five miles, before giving way to her doubts and running back to the cave. But again, Jon was sitting quietly, waiting for her.

Then Kraka was very happy, feeling sure that, at last, she had found a man who could love her despite her foul appearance and even fouler habits, and this time she went all the way to Siglunes, wading through the Eyafjord to reach it, full of determination to catch a shark for her pretty little Jon. And she caught the shark, and came back by the same way.

But Jon had guessed that she would come back once or twice to see if he had run away; and he had seen her peep into the cave, although he had pretended he had not; and he had seen the happiness come over her face on the second occasion. Guessing from this that now she really would go to Siglunes, he crawled from the cave as soon as she was out of sight, and started down the mountain to the farm.

He was not, after his time in Kraka's cave, very steady on his feet, but the dread that Kraka might soon come back kept him moving, and he managed to slip and slide and clamber down from the mountain; and he came in sight of Baldursheim.

Then he heard the sound of heavy, crashing

footsteps behind him as Kraka came running, and her voice shouting, "Wait, Jon! I've got your shark, Jon—and it is a twelve-year-old—nearly a thirteen-year-old! Jon!"

But Jon ran as hard as he could away from her. He reached the farm, and saw the door of the smithy open, and the farmer inside working at his forge. Across the yard Jon ran, in through the smithy door, and round behind the farmer, dropping to his knees and hugging the farmer's legs. The farmer was very surprised by this, and even more surprised when he looked up and saw Kraka's great dark shape blocking most of the light from the doorway; but he saw that it was up to him to deal with the situation. He took a mass of red-hot iron from the fire, and breaking free of his frightened shepherd, he ran at her shouting, "Get out of it, or I'll shove this into you!" Kraka hastily backed away from the forge door when she saw the glowing iron and felt its heat. The farmer followed her. "And now, I charge you, in the name of God the Father, the Son, and the Holy Ghost, never to bother me or my men again." And Kraka, startled and thoroughly alarmed, ran away.

Which shows that it pays to handle trolls, as well as men, firmly; for it is said that Kraka never did attack anyone belonging to Baldursheim again.

Michael Scott's Ride
to Rome

I N THE days when Christendom was ruled from
Rome by the Pope, there lived, in Scotland, a
wizard named Michael Scott. He was a courteous,
quiet man who attended church every Sunday, but,
because in his researches he dealt with devils and
sorcery, there were many who said he was little better
than a devil himself. The wizard ignored such gossip.

Only the Pope, in those days, knew how to
calculate the date of Shrove-tide, and without
knowing that date it was impossible to calculate the
date of any other feast in the year. So, each year, in
every country of Christendom, a man was elected to

travel to Rome, to hear from the Pope's own mouth the date of Shrove-tide, and to bring the knowledge of that date home with him; and in Scotland, one year, the wizard Michael Scott was the man elected to make that journey.

But Michael Scott was busy with other things, some of them having very little to do with Christianity, and the days went by until he realized, suddenly, that it was Candlemas, the last feast of the year, and he had not even thought about his journey to Rome.

Quickly he pulled on a fur-lined gown with a hood, and hurried outside, where he traced a circle and a pentangle in the deep snow. Standing inside the circle he spoke the incantation that would summon up a demon. The demon appeared slowly, forming itself from the air, hating and angry, but trapped by the pentangle.

"If I transformed you into a horse," said the wizard, "how swift would you be?"

"Swift as the wind," said the demon.

"Not swift enough," said the wizard, and dismissed the demon to its own world. He spoke another invocation, and another demon appeared.

"If I transformed you into a horse, how swift would you be?"

"Swifter than the wind."

"You will not do," said Michael Scott; dismissed that demon, called another, and asked it the same question.

"Faster than a sea-gale," said the third demon.

"Of use; but small use;" and the wizard dismissed the third demon and called up a fourth.

"As swift as thought," it said.

"I think even you will hardly be swift enough," said the wizard; but with another spell he turned the demon into a strange, ugly horse, and mounted it. Immediately it leaped from the earth into the sky, whirling the snow into dense white clouds and leaving patches of black night showing through like holes in fabric.

They sped, faster than a breath, high above the land of Scotland, and of England, and the demon said to its rider, "Tell me, Wizard; what do the old women say as they put the fire out at night?"

But Michael Scott knew well enough that the demon was trying to trick him, for the old women said a prayer, and if, in answer, he spoke the words of a Christian prayer to the demon, it would vanish and he would fall through miles of empty air to strike the earth below. So he said only, "Ride on to

Rome, demon, and do not concern yourself with such matters."

But in the space of a blink after, as they passed over the Alps, the demon called out, "Come, Wizard; tell me; what do the mothers say when they put their sweet, sweet little ones to bed?"

The mothers spoke another prayer, and so Michael Scott replied only, "On to Rome, demon; and do not worry yourself about the mothers or their little ones."

A blink after that and they were in Rome; and Michael Scott hurried into the Papal Palace, sending every guard he found running with the news that the messenger from Scotland had at last arrived. The Pope rose from his bed at once and came to see the Wizard; came so quickly that there was still a little unmelted snow on the Wizard's cap; but the Pope was angry and in no mood to be helpful.

"You are late," he said.

"I was busy," said Michael Scott, "but now, at last, I am come."

"There is snow on your cap," said the Pope.

"It is the snow of Scotland," said Michael Scott.

"How can that be?" said the Pope. "I do not believe you. There is some trickery here, and I shall not tell you the date of Shrove-tide until you can

96

prove to me that you come from Scotland."

"I have fetched Your Holiness from your bed, and you have had to dress in haste," said the Wizard.

"That is correct," said the Pope angrily.

"I know," said Michael Scott; "because there is a shoe on your foot which is not your own."

The Pope looked down in surprise and saw, on his left foot, his own shoe; but, on his right foot, a pretty, pointed, embroidered yellow shoe.

Michael Scott said, "Wise men—and I am a wise man—do not ask how the Father of the Holy Church comes to have a woman's shoe upon his foot. I ask, Your Holiness, only to know the date of Shrove-tide."

There was a long silence while the Pope wondered how many cardinals and servants had overheard what the wizard had said. Then he said, "Oh very well—Shrove-tide falls on the first of April."

"What?" said the wizard.

"The first of April!" shouted the Pope.

"Pardon?"

"The first of—Are you deaf?" yelled the Pope.

"No, Your Holiness, but I must be sure, for I am afraid that I will forget the date on the way back to Scotland, and then I will have to come back and – get Your Holiness out of bed again."

"The first Tuesday of the first moon of Spring is Shrove-tide," said the Pope angrily, "and now there is no need for any more devil-dealing Scotsmen to come to my court!"

So Michael Scott bowed himself out of the gracious presence, mounted his demon horse in the courtyard, and, in a breath, flew back to the snows of Britain. As they flew high over the Pennines, the demon said, "Answer me one question, Wizard, if you can; what do women say when they cross themselves?"

"Never mind that, demon," said the Wizard. "Fly straight before you, as I command, and forget about the women."

He finished speaking just as the demon's hoofs struck the ground outside his house, and, as soon as Michael Scott was off its back, the demon vanished, crying, "Good luck to you, Wizard, but curses on your teacher!"

And that was how Michael Scott brought back to Scotland not only the date of Shrove-tide, but the secret of calculating that date; and saved his countrymen the trouble and expense of sending a man to Rome every year.

The New Year Visitors

T HERE were once two brothers who argued over
whether there were such creatures as elves, or
not; the elder said that there certainly were because
he had seen them about the farmhouse just at dusk;
but the younger said that there certainly were not,
because he had never seen them, and that any man
who believed in such things was a fool. This
argument went on for several years, without either
brother being able to feel that he had won, but at
last it broke out in a quarrel so fierce that the
younger brother said that he was unable to tolerate
living with such a half-wit any longer, and he was

going to leave. The elder brother was sorry for this, and worried, and asked him if he would not stay for a day or two longer, to think the matter over, and, when the answer to this was 'no', if he ever intended to return.

"I will not stay another moment in this house with you," said the younger brother, "but if ever I find proof that the elves exist, then I will come back" – which was his way of saying that he never would.

It did not take the younger brother – whose name was Peter – very long to pack his belongings, because he did not own very much; and then he left home, with the dog that had belonged to him since it had been a puppy, and he spent the first night with friends. The next morning he travelled out of the district altogether. He earned his living by going from one farm to another, hiring himself out as a labourer, and delivering packages and messages. He spent several years in this way, for although it was a hard life and not much to his taste, he was too proud to go back to his brother.

It happened that, one New Year's Eve, he came to a farmhouse where he had never been before. He went up to the door, thinking that they would not refuse him hospitality on the night of a festival, but he found all the people of the house in a sullen, melancholy mood, and no preparations seemed to have been made for celebrating the arrival of the New Year. True, they invited him in, and allowed his dog to come in too, and gave them both a place by the fire, and food and drink, but they didn't seem capable of smiling. After eating his food somewhat guiltily, without hearing a word spoken, Peter asked the people why they were so gloomy. He was told that it was because they all wanted to go to the midnight church-service for the New Year, but that they could not leave the house empty for fear of thieves or fire, and that no one dared to stay behind in the house because, on three previous New Year's Eves, the church-goers had returned to find the watchers dead, with all their bones broken.

"*All* their bones broken?" said Peter.

"All their bones broken."

"For three years running?"

"Each New Year's Eve for the past three years. Something terrible has been visiting this house on that night. Perhaps it will not come while we are all here, but we dare not leave one of our number here alone."

Peter sat quietly by the fire after this, unable to stop wondering what it was that visited the house on the last night of every old year. He began to think of a way that he might stay in the house and see what it was, and still survive. He looked at the walls of the room, which were of wooden panelling, and he left his seat and examined them, and then said, "You can go to your church-service, all of you, if you will trust me to guard your house. I am an honest man, and I assure you that I will not rob you."

"What?" said the farmer. "Do you mean to say that you would stay here, after what we have told you?"

"Yes," said Peter. "I am very curious to see what it is that can break all the bones in a man's body—and you need not be concerned. It is my own choice, and I am a stranger to you, so if I go the same way as the others, it will be no great sorrow to you." And since this was true, and since everyone there wanted very much to go to the church-service, he quickly persuaded them, and they all put on coats or shawls, and went out, leaving the house to him.

As soon as they had gone, Peter jumped up and searched the house for tools, with his dog running excitedly after him from place to place. He searched hurriedly, for he could not tell when the thing that broke bones would come. He found a claw-hammer and a strong, broad-bladed chisel, and, using these tools, he pried a part of the panelling loose and squeezed in behind it. He pulled the panelling roughly back into place, and hoped that he was well enough hidden. His dog ran about near the panelling, and whined anxiously, but there was barely room in his hiding-place for Peter, so he could not take his dog in with him. After a while, the dog lay down in the middle of the room, with one eye fixed sadly on the spot where his master had disappeared. Peter made a hole in the panelling with the chisel, so that he could peer into the room with one eye.

He waited and, a very few minutes after he had made his peephole, he heard a chatter of voices, and a crash as the door of the farmhouse was thrown open, and a rush and rattle of many running feet on the kitchen's wooden floor. He put his eye to the peephole and saw his poor dog snatched from his resting-place and thrown down so hard that every bone in his body might well be broken. Peter was so shocked and afraid that he shut his eyes, and saw nothing more until he heard voices saying that there was a smell of human flesh about the place. Then he opened one eye and looked through the peephole again, and saw many little people, none of them more than four feet high, but so solid and strong, and so ugly, fierce and malicious in appearance that the very sight of them frightened him, and made him wish devoutly that he had never doubted the existence of elves, or volunteered to guard the farmhouse. The elves were snuffing the air for his smell and he was afraid that they would soon drag him from his hiding place and break all his bones too.

But then one of the elves said, "You should not be surprised at there being a smell of human flesh about the place when humans live here all the year round and have left within the hour."

All the elves took deep breaths of relief, and let them out with grunts and whistles; but they were not more relieved than the man hiding behind the panelling. He watched through his peephole as the elves pushed aside all the furniture of the farmhouse and set up, in the middle of the room, a small table of their own. Over this they spread a beautiful white cloth with a thick, heavy hem of embroidery worked in gold; and they laid the table with bowls, plates, cups, jugs, spoons and knives, all of silver. But before they sat down to eat the feast which Peter could smell being prepared on the farmhouse fire, they sent one of the young elves to stand watch by the door; and as soon as they had finished eating, they called out to him, "How does the night go?"

The young elf poked his head round the door and said, "There's plenty of time yet."

The meal over, the table was cleared and all the fine vessels and utensils, and the wonderful cloth, were packed away. Then two of the elves, a man and a woman, stepped forward side by side, and another man-elf stepped in front of them, and spoke some words before calling out to the young elf, "How does the night go?"

"There's plenty of time yet," said the young elf.

Then all the elves began to sing, and they made a strange, high, creeping noise, until all the hair on Peter's body stood on end and prickled. He could only imagine that the elves were celebrating a marriage.

When the singing was over, the young elf at the door was again asked how the night was going, and he again replied that there was plenty of time; and then the elves began to dance, with much stamping of feet, clapping of hands, shouting and loud music. This dancing went on for a long time, but at last they stopped, and one of them called out, "Door-keeper! How goes the night?"

"Oh, there's still one more watch," said the young elf, looking in.

At this, saying a prayer within himself, Peter

105

shouted, as loudly as he could, "You liar! It's daylight already!"

The elves were startled by the loud voice, but could only suppose it to be one of themselves who had spoken, and what the voice said panicked them so that they rushed about the room, scratching and chittering like rats, and humming like bees.

"I'll teach you to mind your watch!" cried one of the biggest elves, and, seizing the young elf who had been the doorkeeper, he threw him down on the floor and broke all his bones. Then, pulling open the door, all the angry elves rushed out all together, in a pack, leaving their belongings behind. Peter pushed his way out from behind the panelling and ran after them, and was just in time to see them jump, all together, into a lake not far from the farmyard.

Peter ran back to the farmhouse, threw the body of the dead elf outside, pushed the furniture back into place, gathered up everything that the elves had left and hid it in a corner; and then sat down by the fire with the farmer's Bible in his hands, in case the elves decided to come back for their property.

Soon after, the people of the farm came back from the church-service and, finding Peter sitting comfortably by the fire, asked if he had kept watch as he had promised to do.

"I did; and there was something to see," Peter said; and he went on to tell them everything that had happened, and fetched out the treasure that the elves had left behind, and his poor dog, to show them. "But I am afraid I have damaged your panelling," he said.

"Never mind the panelling," said the farmer. "You have discovered what it is that visits us on New Year's Eve; and I think that is worth a little chipped panelling." And the farmer and his wife wanted Peter to take all the elvish treasure; but Peter would not agree to this. He kept the wonderful, gold embroidered cloth for himself, since it would have been a pity to rip it in half; but the rest of the treasure he divided fairly between himself and the farmer. Even half of the treasure was enough to make him a rich man.

Then he went home to his brother and told him that he would never again doubt the existence of elves, or call his elders half-wits for believing in them; but he did not stay with his brother. With his half of the treasure he bought his own farm, and was a rich, and lucky, man until the day he died. It is also said that the elves never visited again the farm where he had won his treasure.

Pan Twerdowski

Four hundred years ago, in Poland, there lived a wizard, a nobleman who had wasted all his fortune in the practice of alchemy and witchcraft, medicine and astrology. His name was Pan Twerdowski. He wanted to discover the Alchemist's stone which would turn all base metal to pure gold; the Healer's stone which would cure all disease; and the Elixir which would give him immortal life—for Twerdowski had so much to do, to learn, to discover, that above all things he feared that death would interrupt him. As he grew older, the fear grew stronger, and, at last, he decided to make a bargain for his life. Using his great knowledge of witchcraft, he marked out circles and pentagrams on the floor in salt; he lit braziers and threw bitter, stinking herbs into them; he cast a spell with a black knife; and he summoned the Devil from Hell and made a pact with him.

They spent some hours in hard bargaining. Twerdowski wanted immortality; the Devil wanted his soul: but, finally, it was agreed that Twerdowski should have twenty-four more years of life, that during all that time the Devil should perform any task Twerdowski ordered, and answer any questions he asked; and that, at the end of that time, the Devil could collect Twerdowski's soul and body, and do with them as he pleased—but only if the body and soul were collected from Rome. This was agreed to on both sides, a contract was drawn up, and Twerdowski signed it, in his own blood, with his longest finger. And as soon as he had drawn the last letter of his name, he felt new strength come into his old body. He looked into a mirror; his hair was darker, and his face younger. He could work for longer than ever in his laboratory, and would have the Devil's help in his researches—but he found that, now he had the immortality he had always wanted, for he was sure that he would find some way of escaping the contract, he had lost interest in the sciences he had always loved. Instead he spent his time in gathering wealth or playing tricks, and the only questions he asked were idly curious ones. He ordered the Devil to bring all the silver in Poland to one place, and cover it over with sand to hide it; and he demanded from the Devil the power to change sand into gold by running it through his fingers; and in revenge for a snub given him by one man he destroyed a whole village, by holding a little magnifying glass over its name on a map and letting the sun shine through the glass until both name and village were burned; and in the town of Krakov people began to tell of having seen Twerdowski flying overhead on the back of a giant cockerel, or, sometimes, of Twerdowski flying by himself, without any wings at all to hold him up. But, though Twerdowski seemed to grow no older, time went on passing, and the twenty-four years came to an end. Once they were over, they seemed not to have lasted for twenty-four hours and Twerdowski wondered if he were really clever enough to save himself from the Devil, and shuddered, and wondered now what he had gained by selling his soul that was worth suffering the pains of Hell for; but he comforted himself by repeating over the clause in the contract which stipulated that the Devil could only collect his payment in Rome; and Twerdowski had no intention, and had never had any intention, of going to Rome.

On the day that his contract with the Devil ran out, Twerdowski went for a long walk in the pine forests on his estate; and he lay down beneath a tall pine tree, to rest and enjoy the forest and its scents for what might be the last time. One second after the exact mark of the clock on which, twenty-four years before, Twerdowski had signed the contract, the Devil appeared, and said, "I have been to Rome, and you were not there. Where were you?"

"I was here," said Pan Twerdowski.

"Why were you not in Rome, as you contracted to be?" demanded the Devil.

"Because I do not mean to give up my soul or my body to you."

"You must go to Rome, and you shall," said the Devil. "Order your coach at once; send messengers ahead to open the frontiers and hire a ship—or climb on my back, and I will carry you there in a moment!"

"No," said Pan Twerdowski. "I shall not go to Rome with you, nor alone, nor with anything human or inhuman. I shall stay here, and never die, for my soul is yours alone, and you cannot have it."

"If you will not go willingly, I shall beat you there!" said the Devil.

"Beat away," said Pan Twerdowski; "it cannot be as bad as Hell."

So the Devil uprooted a pine-tree, and began to beat Twerdowski with it, trying to drive him to Rome as an animal is driven, but though it was a terrible beating, though he was black with bruises, and bleeding, Twerdowski would not move an inch, but only cried, again and again, "It cannot be as bad as Hell!"

After a long while the Devil was exhausted, threw down the pine-tree, and went away, wrapped in an angry storm. Twerdowski could not move from where he lay, and he sobbed, "It was not as bad as Hell," into the pine-needles, until some of his servants found him. They hardly recognised him, but they carried him home and put him to bed, and there he stayed for many months, recovering. But the Devil did not come to him, and Twerdowski began to think that he, and he only in all the history of the world, had outwitted Satan, and he flattered himself that he was a very clever man indeed.

When he got up from his bed, his bruises had faded and his wounds had healed, but he was a very old man, and he had lost his magical powers. His gold had turned to sand again, and he could not reach the silver he had buried, and it is still there, where the Devil buried it for him, at Olkusz, but now it is being mined. Twerdowski turned to his old researches again, and he earned his living as a doctor. He was skilled in medicine, and he became known as an excellent physician, although people were always a little afraid of him. He became so famous that, one day, the servant of another doctor came to him, bringing a message from his master: Would Twerdowski come to him and give him his advice on a very difficult case? Twerdowski was very flattered by this compliment to his skill, and he willingly travelled with the servant to a village some miles away, eager to meet this colleague who thought so highly of him.

They reached the village, and the servant led Twerdowski to the inn where the doctor was staying, and went off to find his master, leaving Twerdowski to wait in the inn parlour. Twerdowski sat himself at a table close by a bench on which a baby lay in a basket, and from where he sat he could look through a window on the other side of the room, and see the inn's sign swinging to and fro. He could also see a great many ravens; scores and scores of the black birds were gathering about the inn, landing on its roof and the roofs of the buildings near by; but they were not making a sound.

But then the doctor who had sent for him came in. He was dressed in a long black gown and a three-cornered hat. "Aah, Twerdowski," he said pleasantly, and crossed the room, his hand held out to take Twerdowski's. The old man stood up, ready to shake hands, but all the ravens overhead and outside began to croak and scream, and, looking closely at the doctor, Twerdowski saw, poking through his three-cornered hat, the tip of a white horn. Twerdowski turned his eyes to the window and the inn's sign. The inn was called 'Rome'. At once Twerdowski stooped and snatched up the sleeping baby, and the Devil, who had been just about to seize him, drew back hurriedly, for the baby was innocent, and the Devil could not touch the innocent.

"Oh, Twerdowski," said the Devil. " '*Verbum nobile debet esse stabile*' "—a nobleman never goes back on his word.

Then Twerdowski was bitterly ashamed that, in seeking to escape the debt which, eventually, he must pay, he had forgotten even his nobility, and had been prepared to endanger a baby's life rather than give up his own. He laid the baby down, and the Devil snatched him up, and carried him away through the roof.

All the ravens flew into the air around them in a living, beating, screeching black cloud, but the Devil and Twerdowski rushed upwards, beyond them, into air that was freezing cold. Looking down, Twerdowski saw the world shrinking, saw the villages shrinking into dots, saw the forests where he had walked, the fields, the hills, even Poland itself, shrinking into pinpricks, and vanishing. He began to cry, for he had loved his life on earth; and as the world grew smaller still, and all about him grew colder and emptier, and as his memory ran about among the things he had seen and done, he suddenly began to sing, without knowing it, a hymn he had learned as a small boy, a hymn in praise of the Virgin Mary.

His voice was strong, and in the cold and darkness it sounded sharp and clear; and it was forced back to the earth by the speed of their ascent. It echoed from earth's mountains, and crossed valleys, and the people in the towns and villages heard it and came out into the streets to listen; farmers, and shepherds, travelling-people and fishermen, all heard the singing, and all listened, holding their breath, and looking up into the black sky, and at the white stars. They were afraid, and the hair prickled at the back of their necks, but it was a fear filled with beauty and longing, and many of them wept. "Whoever it is that sings has been wicked," they said, "but he repents, and will be saved." And, as they listened, the song in the darkness brought them the certainty that they, too, would be saved, and they were comforted.

Twerdowski, as he ended the hymn, though still in the Devil's grip, heard a voice say, "Twerdowski; you have cleansed my people's souls for me; therefore you shall not go to Hell—but neither can you return to the Earth. You must wait where you can for the Day of Judgement."

When he heard this voice, the Devil at once let go of Twerdowski, and the wizard fell down the sky until, by luck, he landed on a horn of the crescent moon; and there he sits still, waiting for Judgement, and sometimes singing the hymns he remembers from his childhood; but these days his voice is very seldom heard.

Lutey and the Mermaid

I N CUREY, in Cornwall, there once lived a man
named Lutey. He made his living, in the main, as
a fisherman, although he grew vegetables in a small
garden beside his cottage, and was not above
robbing a wrecked ship, coming home with oranges
and lemons in his shirt, or rolling a cask of doubly-
salted butter along the beach, or carrying a small keg
of wine on his shoulder. Sometimes, too, he would
bring home a half-drowned passenger or ship's boy,
for although quick to make a profit out of the
disaster if he could, he was a kind man, who always

gave what help he could to anyone in trouble.

One day, after a bad storm, Lutey was wandering along the beach, looking to see if the storm had washed up anything worth bending down to pick up, since the sea was still too rough for him to go fishing. His little mongrel dog was running in circles round him, coming back whenever he saw his master stop, to sniff at what had been found. Lutey picked up a couple of coins, and some bottles which he thought he would wash out and sell, and then, in a pool of sea-water formed by some rocks, he found a mermaid. He stood and looked at her for a long time, while his dog yapped from a safe distance. Lutey knew that she was a mermaid by the long, strong, coiling tail, all silver and blue, which formed her body from the waist down. Above the waist —well; she was more beautiful than the most beautiful woman Lutey had ever seen. His own wife had been pretty enough for anyone when he had married her, but even combed and washed, and dressed in her best, she had not looked like this creature. His wife's skin was brown and red; the mermaid's was white, absolutely white; as white as the full moon on a clear night. His wife's eyes and hair were dark brown, like his own; the mermaid's hair was almost as white as her skin, but as the wind lifted first one strand and then another, green and blue and yellow lights flickered through it; and her eyes were large and grey. Over all the years Lutey's wife had grown stocky and almost shapeless with keeping house for him, and having his children; and although, when he had married her, Lutey had known this would happen, and although he loved her none the less for it, yet he was held by the sight of the mermaid's heart-breakingly slender arms and neck, and he shook his head in wonder and astonishment, and hoped that he would never forget one line or colour of the sight.

At last the mermaid, who had been staring at him and winding long strands of her hair round her fingers, stretched out her beautiful arms to him, and said, "The storm washed me up here, lad; wouldst carry me back?"

Lutey started at the sound of her voice, but then grinned through his beard, and said, "Aye; I reckon I could carry a little thing like thee down to the water, even if it is a mile out;" and he climbed into the pool, and lifted the mermaid in his arms. She put her arms about his neck, coiled her long tail round his waist, and laid her head against his shoulder. "Parson wouldn't like this if he could see it," Lutey said, "but he can't, and I shan't tell him." And he began to carry the mermaid over the long stretch of sand to the sea's edge. His little dog ran after him.

"Thou'rt a good man," said the mermaid, and rubbed her cold cheek against his beard. "If I could grant wishes, and I said I would give thee three, what wouldst wish for, lad?"

"That would take some thinking about," Lutey said.

"Think, then, love," said the mermaid.

"Well . . ." said Lutey. "Well . . . there's a lot suffer from aches and pains, especially in this cold weather. I know my poor old gel does, and it catches me sharp sometimes, in the back, when I bend— and then there's fevers, and coughs and colds and all sorts. Aye; I reckon I'd wish for the power to heal if I was going to wish. That'd do some good for a lot of folk, that would."

"And the second wish?"

"Well . . . folk lose a lot of things, and most of 'em bain't got that much that they can afford to lose it; so I'd wish next for the power to discover things lost. That'd be a help."

"And the third wish, love?"

"Well . . . Those other wishes wouldn't be much help if they died with me, would they? Not that I'm old, but I'm getting on. So, I'd wish that the powers could pass down to my sons and daughters. Aye; that I would."

He felt a coldness on his cheek as the mermaid kissed him. "Thou'rt a good man," she said. "As good as thou'rt handsome." And she kissed him three times more; on the eyelid, on the neck and on the lips.

"Hey, hey, hey," Lutey said. "Madam! I hope my old gel bain't looking this way. I got to go back to her, tha knowst."

"Come with me instead," said the mermaid, and clung to him more tightly. "Come with me, love. You sail over the water in your boats, you men; hast never wondered what lies beneath it? Deep, deep beneath?"

"I have wondered," said Lutey; "but I should drown."

"I wouldn't let thee drown, lad," said the mermaid. "I'd take thee where no man that breathes air has ever been; and I'd love thee."

Lutey reached the edge of the sea, and, shaking his head, he waded into it, carrying the mermaid to where the water was deep enough for her to swim away. "I can't come," he said.

The mermaid tightened her arms and tail about him with frightening strength. "Come with me, and

be my love," she said. "Come with me and see the
sunken ships with their sails all torn into rags and
drifting with the tides; come and see what they were
carrying, all spilt, all spoilt; come and search for
coins in the sand down there, Lutey, my Handsome;
come and dig for lost rings and broken necklaces;
and for every precious stone you find, I'll give you
another kiss." And she kissed him again, with a
touch even colder than before; a cold that struck
him through, and yet was strangely pleasant, excit-
ing; thrilling. And if he had wondered before what
lay beneath the sea and its changing colours, now he
wondered and longed to know, ten times more.

"Why stay here above the lovely water?" the
mermaid asked, as she stroked his hair. "Why suffer
the storms and the pains; why work and worry, and
run after every little thing that might put a crumb in
your mouth? We don't live so under the sea: we
never worry about what might happen; we never
worry about food; we have no needs. Let go, my
love; let go of your sorry world; come with me; sink
with me into the darkness. Oh come with me,
Lutey; come with me, love; be my love, Sweet; come
with me."

Lutey shivered as her cold kisses stole the
strength from him, and he sank to his knees in the

water. The sea rushed up against his chest and splashed about the mermaid. He opened his mouth, and was about to say that he would go with her, when, from the edge of the sea came the sound of his little dog barking. The mermaid, startled, loosened her hold, and Lutey looked round.

Beyond the noisy little dog he saw the beach he had walked along that morning; and beyond the beach he saw the small, poor cottage where he lived. He saw smoke rising from the holes in the roof; he saw his wife in the vegetable garden, stooping to pull something up; and he saw three of his children running, one after another, on to the beach. He knew then that he could not go with the mermaid, and he felt such sorrow at that, and for the dwindling, wasted life of his wife, and for the lives of his children which were yet to waste, that he felt a pain as if a knife had been driven into him, and tears came into his eyes. "Oh, Sea-maid," he said. "I would come—I would come—but look, dost see my old gel back there? My poor old gel; if I go with thee, who's to dig the garden for her when her back aches, and get the vegetables in for next year? See the holes in the roof? Who'd mend 'em? See the smoke? Who'd chop the wood for the fire? Who'd find the money to feed and clothe the little uns if I wasn't here? No; my old gel, she's too old now to do any better for herself than me, and I've got to stay and look after her."

The mermaid wrapped her arms tightly round his neck, lashed out with her tail, and dragged him beneath the water. But Lutey was a strong man, and the water was not yet very deep. He struggled, and brought his head into the air again; and he dragged his knife from his belt and held it before the mermaid's face, knowing that all such creatures are afraid of cold iron; and he said, "Go, in God's name!"

The water turned foamy and white all round him as the mermaid swam away; but at a distance she rose from the water again, and she called, "Thou'rt a good man, Lutey, and each one of thy three wishes shall be granted. I prophesy, too, that neither thee nor any of thy children, nor thy children's children, nor any born of thy line shall ever, from this day, be hungry or cold. But thou art mine, Lutey, and I shall have thee. I grant thee nine more years to live in the air, and then I shall come and fetch thee home, lad." Then she sank beneath the water, and Lutey waded back from the sea to his family.

Within a few days he had a chance to test the truth of the mermaid's words, for his youngest child fell sick, and could not sleep; but after Lutey had stroked her head and kissed her, she did sleep, and woke cured. It soon spread, from house to house, and village to village, that Lutey of Curey could heal, and people began to come to him when they were in pain, or feverish, or had wounds which had turned bad, or sores, or coughing-fits; and Lutey's skill and touch always brought ease. When it became known that he could also discover things that were lost, still more people came to him, and they all brought payment in eggs, or cake, or milk, or cheese, and sometimes in money, fulfilling the mermaid's prophecy that Lutey's children would never again be cold or hungry.

On the ninth anniversary of the day he had found the mermaid, Lutey went fishing, taking with him one of his youngest sons, a boy barely eight years old, who already possessed some of his father's powers. They fished all day, made a good catch, and, as the light was beginning to fade, and they were thinking of putting back to shore, the mermaid suddenly rose from the water near the boat, stretched out her lovely arms, and called Lutey's name.

Lutey immediately stood, and moved as though to jump overboard. His son, though very frightened, was quick enough to reach out and clutch at his father's legs. Lutey looked down at him impatiently. "I stayed then," he said. "Now let me go." The boy released him in bewilderment, and Lutey threw himself into the sea. He sank, and did not rise, for the mermaid dragged him down with her.

Lutey's son was left alone in the still rocking boat, the air growing cold and dark over the sea. He rowed home alone without his father, and no trace of Lutey was ever seen after that; neither his body, nor his clothes, nor anything belonging to him was ever washed up for mortals to find.

Lutey's son grew, and came into all the powers his father had had; and others of his own, for after he had seen the mermaid take his father, he always looked so hard for what was not to be seen that at last he saw its shadows——moving shadows at the edges and corners of rooms; shadows among trees and stone field-walls of the land, and among the rocks of the beach; shadows miming what was yet to happen.

But he never lived to have children, this second-sighted Lutey, for he still followed his father's trade of fisherman, and nine years after his father's disappearance, he went fishing with his younger brother; and the mermaid rose from the water and called to him. Without a word, without any hesitation, Young Lutey swung himself over the boat's side into her arms, and sank with her into the deep, cold sea.

His brother lived to marry, and his children inherited the family's gifts, as did their children, and indeed, for many generations there were no healers in Cornwall so famous as the Luteys of Curey; but every nine years the mermaid rose from the water and called for her payment; and another Lutey was drowned.

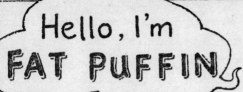